CHICAGO
O'HARE
INTERNATIONAL
AIRPORT

WORLD'S BUSIEST,
WORLD'S BEST

CHICAGO O'HARE INTERNATIONAL AIRPORT

WORLD'S BUSIEST, WORLD'S BEST

BY JOSEPH P. HOWARD

To my wife, Dee,
for her support and encouragement,
and my family, Lisa, Joe, Jennifer,
Mike, Kathy, Colleen, and Tim.
With special thanks to Michael and
Robert Bullington, Ed Walsh,
and so many others who helped.

ISBN: 1-882933-13-3

President . . . . Jack C. Cherbo

Vice President . . . . Elaine Hoffman

Editorial Director . . . . .Tina G. Rubin

Profiles Director . . . . Liza Yetenekian Smith

Contributing Editors . . . .
           Christina M. Beausang, Linda Chase

Author . . . . Joseph P. Howard

Profiles Writer . . . . Stan Ziemba

Designer . . . . Christine Motley

Contributing Designer . . . . . . Mika Toyoura

Photo Editor . . . . Robin Sterling

Production Coordinator . . . Ellen Kettenbeil

Sales Administration . . . . Joan Baker

Administrative Assistant . . . Rejyna Douglass

Midwestern Regional
Manager . . . . Merle Gratton

Publishers Representative . . . . . .Tim Burke

Front and back covers: Peter J. Schulz,
City of Chicago, Dept. of Aviation

1997 Cherbo Publishing Group, Inc.

Acknowledgments

The author extends his appreciation to Lisa Howard, former director of public relations for the Department of Aviation, and her staff for providing access to documents and records, as well as allowing the author to visit and observe regions of the airport beyond the terminals, areas that the average traveler never sees.

The author also thanks the following persons for their assistance along the way: Lou Eberhardt, Maria Healy, Ed Walsh, John Hoellen, Alderman Bernard Stone, and Harold Schultz.

PHOTO BY JAMES BLANK©

Contents

PHOTO BY PETER J. SCHULZ,
CITY OF CHICAGO, DEPARTMENT
OF AVIATION

PART ONE

Reaching for the Sky

Introduction

ifty years ago, the blueprint for an airport was drawn on the grounds of an abandoned aircraft plant on the edge of Chicago. Thus began Chicago O'Hare International Airport, whose fame would eventually reach across the globe. Presidents, prime ministers, a pope, emperors, kings, queens, celebrities, and millions of ordinary travelers have passed through the doors of its 7,700-acre domain. To those who love aviation, O'Hare is a rare beauty, a legend that bears the name of a legend.

O'Hare was named for Edward H. "Butch" O'Hare, a naval air hero who died in the South Pacific in the early days of World War II. Butch O'Hare was born in St. Louis, but Chicago claimed him — simply because he lived there for a time. How long a time? Long enough for Chicago's aldermen. In their proclamation naming the airport in his honor, they unabashedly called him a Chicago boy.

In 1961, Chicago's O'Hare captured the crown of the world's busiest airport — quite an achievement when one considers its humble beginnings.

In the 1930s, the expanse where the airport stands today was known as Orchard Place, a rural area on the northwest edge of Chicago dotted with farms, orchards, a golf course, churches, and a tiny airstrip.

During World War II, Orchard Place was chosen as a site for Douglas Aircraft Company to build cargo planes for the military. The first C-54 Skymaster rolled off the assembly line at Orchard Place in July 1943. Two years later, with the war winding down, production was halted, and Douglas Field settled into limbo.

When the war ended, returning servicemen who had "seen the world" no longer confined them-

ABOVE: O'HARE'S SLEEK, $618 MILLION INTERNATIONAL TERMINAL WAS BUILT AT NO COST TO TAXPAYERS. *PHOTO BY PETER J. SCHULZ, CITY OF CHICAGO, DEPT. OF AVIATION. OPPOSITE: A UNITED AIRCRAFT WAITS ON THE TARMAC AT O'HARE IN SEPTEMBER 1955. PHOTO COURTESY OF UNITED AIRLINES*

selves to the towns and cities where they were born. Americans were suddenly on the move, and the transportation industry, preparing for a postwar travel boom, watched inventive new airline companies challenge the railroads.

In Chicago, the nation's railroad center, a love affair with the flying machine had blossomed decades earlier. In 1945, Municipal Airport, the city's first official airport, was handling more than a million passengers a year. City fathers foresaw the need for a second airport, a new, bigger one that would accommodate the jetliners of the future.

Chicago explored several sites, but had its eye on the idle Douglas plant on the northwest side of the city. Mayor Edward J. Kelly made inquiries in Washington, and in March 1946, the federal government — no longer in need of "defense plants" — handed over the Douglas property and its 1,080 acres to the city. The seed of a great airport had been planted.

From the onset, this was to be no ordinary airport. Big, busy, and determined, O'Hare was destined to reach out to the nation and the world — despite the obstacles that would spring up along the way.

Today the land bears little resemblance to the rural locale that was Orchard Place. Jumbo jets rumble across concrete runways where corn and soybeans once grew. Mammoth hangars service jetliners and cargo planes in the very spot where farmhouses once stood. Beyond O'Hare's fences, business and industry are flourishing due to the presence of this remarkable airport.

Building this giant complex was no small task. The story of O'Hare Airport reveals the vision of Chicago's leaders as well as the airlines who created this airport — and finally, the dedication of those who carry on its work.

PART ONE
Reaching for the Sky

Chapter One

That Travelin' Town

On a sunny day in March 1963, a cheer arose from some 6,000 people at Chicago O'Hare International Airport. Across the field, the presidential jet, *The Caroline,* had touched down on the runway.

The president of the United States, John F. Kennedy, had arrived in the city to dedicate the airport named in honor of Lieutenant Commander Edward (Butch) O'Hare, a navy air hero of World War II.

"Welcome to Chicago, Mr. President," Mayor Richard J. Daley said. When the handshakes and greetings ended, civic officials and dignitaries smiled with pride as President Kennedy delivered an appraisal of the scene before him.

"This is an extraordinary airport, an extraordinary city, and an extraordinary country." The crowd applauded. Mayor Daley, Governor Otto Kerner, Senator Paul Douglas, and a host of city officials beamed. President Kennedy called O'Hare Airport "one of the wonders of the modern world" and marveled that in five years O'Hare had vaulted from the 16th most active airport in America to the first.

"There is no other airport in the world which serves so many people and so many airplanes," Kennedy declared.

Today, almost 34 years later, the late president's assessment rings as true as it did in 1963. O'Hare International Airport, a sprawling giant covering 7,700 acres of land on the northwest side of Chicago, is a modern facility extending a warm welcome to more than 67.2 million travelers a year, the busiest airport in the world.

How does an airport achieve such numbers? Some say the answer lies in its location, but in O'Hare International's case, its success transcends location alone. The rank and reputation of the airport can be traced to the bold vision of those who created it and the dedication of those who operate it today.

Chicago's Department of Aviation at one time included three airports: O'Hare International on the city's northwest side; Midway Airport on the southwest side; and Meigs Field on the lakefront — all

OPPOSITE: LIEUTENANT COMMANDER EDWARD "BUTCH" O'HARE IS READY FOR TAKEOFF, CIRCA 1943. THE AIRPORT BEARS THE NAME OF THE WORLD WAR II NAVAL AIR ACE. *PHOTO: CHICAGO HISTORICAL SOCIETY*

committed to serving business, industry, and the traveling public. Today, O'Hare International reigns as the crown jewel in the city's aviation system, a world-class port in the heart of America.

"Chicago has always been a crossroads of American transportation," President Kennedy said on that day in 1963. "Now, Chicago is becoming a crossroads for the world as well."

Chicago reigns as the logical and natural hub for the aviation industry, not only because of its size but because of its geographical location and ranking as the major port of commerce and industry between the East and West coasts.

During the heyday of the railroads, Chicago was known as America's railroad center. Each day, fabled trains with fabled names — the *Broadway Limited,* the *Green Diamond,* the *Golden State Limited ,* the *Panama Limited,* the *Twin City Zephyr,* and the *Hiawatha* — rumbled in and out of depots that looked more like Greek temples than railroad stations.

This golden age of travel lasted almost a century and a half. The railroad was king. No wonder few people gave more than passing notice in 1903 when two brothers from Dayton, Ohio, successfully tested a flying machine at Kitty Hawk, North Carolina. Yet the airships developed in the wake of the Wright Brothers' invention would one day send the railroad into the realm of nostalgia.

In a few short years, aviation's trailblazers spread the gospel of flight across America, and Chicago was quickly caught up in the

romance. One of the first to arrive in the Midwest was a pilot named Glenn Curtiss. In October 1909, while thousands watched, he executed three short flights from Hawthorne Racetrack southwest of Chicago and was credited with Illinois' first recorded airplane flights. His aerial feats inspired local entrepreneurs.

Working in a southside garage, Charles Bates manufactured an aero engine, mounted it on a flying machine, and hauled it to Washington Park for a demonstration. Instructor Max Lillie opened a school in Chicago in 1911 and taught the mastery of flight to those daring enough to enroll. One of his pupils was Katherine "Kitty" Stinson, the first woman to enter a major flying meet.

In 1912, an aviator named Farnum Fish loaded bolts of cloth, letters, and 7,500 handbills aboard a plane in Chicago and took off for Milwaukee, some 90 miles away. Before landing, Fish banked his

plane and scattered the handbills over the city. His flight time was two hours and six minutes.

By 1918, the flying machine, now called the airplane, had literally taken off, not only in America but abroad as well. Technology had advanced in giant steps. New planes gracing the skies bore little resemblance to the primitive machine the Wright Brothers had flown at Kitty Hawk. These new birds flew faster, higher, and longer, and had already found new applications.

When World War I erupted in Europe in 1914, the major adversaries broadened the battlefield to include the skies. America, while still on the sideline, prepared itself for war on the ground and in the air.

Philip K. Wrigley, a navy chief machinist's mate who later became a chewing gum magnate, headed the country's first school of aviation mechanics in 1917 at the Great Lakes Naval Training Center north of Chicago.

During the war, aerial combat made its debut in an unsophisticated fashion as enemies shot it out in the sky with pistols and rifles. After aircraft designers mounted machine guns on planes, scores of aircraft engaged in dogfights high above the trenches.

In those early days of air warfare, Major General William Brancker of the British Air Council wryly commented, "War has been the making of aviation."

The Making of Aviation

That may have been true, but back in America, an unlikely agency was stimulating the growth of civil aviation: the United States Postal Service, which launched its first regularly scheduled airmail service in May 1918 from a polo field in Washington, D.C., to Belmont Park

LEFT: FLIGHT INSTRUCTOR MAX LILLIE AND KATHERINE STINSON, CIRCA 1911. ABOVE: AN AERIAL VIEW OF MUNICIPAL AIRPORT, 1932. *PHOTOS: CHICAGO HISTORICAL SOCIETY*

Racetrack in New York. The army supplied the postal service with a small fleet of two-seater Curtiss Jenny biplanes and pilots to fly them.

Later that month, a biplane carried mail on the 350-mile trip from Cleveland to Chicago in 133 minutes. And just east of Michigan Avenue near Chicago's lakefront, pilot Trent C. Fry lifted off in a plane from Grant Park, one of the city's first airmail landing fields, with 450 pounds of mail, landed in Bryan, Ohio, and exchanged mail with another pilot. Fry rested five

ground crew at White City under arrest. Outraged city officials assembled after the accident and vowed that flights above the city had to be ended. Alderman Anton J. Cermak, a future mayor, introduced a resolution to prohibit all aircraft from flying over the city.

Yet in the heat of the moment, a cooler head prevailed. Alderman Guy Guernsey convinced Cermak to modify his resolution from "prohibit" to "regulate," telling his colleague in a voice filled with empathy and resignation, "Aviation is here to stay." Hopefully, it would be safer.

As tragic as the crash was, it did little to dampen the public's ardor for the machines that appeared regularly in the skies.

Against All Odds

Take the story of Bessie Coleman, a young black woman working as a manicurist in a Chicago beauty salon at the time of the blimp accident. Like other young people, Bessie was fascinated with flying machines and one day informed her mother she had reached a decision, one that would change her life.

"Bessie has lost her mind," her mother lamented. "She is going to fly airplanes!" Indeed she was.

Bessie's first obstacle was finding a teacher. Flying schools wanted no part of her. In that day, it was bad enough allowing a woman to vote, but unheard of allowing a woman — and a black woman at that — to fly.

But Bessie Coleman was determined. She traveled to Europe and

minutes and returned to Chicago, clipping five hours off the running time by train. In September, Max Miller, a postal service pilot, flew from Long Island, New York, to Grant Park with a load of mail, arriving in under 10 hours.

From Chicago's lakefront to the amusement park known as White City at 63rd and South Park Way and to parks and racetracks around the city, the sight of airplanes, barnstorming stunt pilots, balloons, and dirigibles overhead captured the imagination of the crowds. On the evening of July 21, 1919, however, a spectacular disaster in downtown Chicago gave many people second thoughts about the "goings on" in the skies above them.

At 5 p.m., homeward-bound workers craned their necks to watch a Goodyear blimp from White City meandering above the city's downtown (the Loop). Someone recalled seeing a tiny spurt of flame coming from the dirigible. The next moment the dirigible was engulfed in flames. Crowds in the streets below screamed in horror. Four of the five crewmen parachuted from the blimp as it descended in a ball of fire and crashed through the skylight of the Illinois Trust and Savings Bank at Jackson Boulevard and LaSalle Street.

Thirteen people, including a crewman from the blimp and a number of bank clerks, stenographers, and messengers, were killed. More than 100 others were injured. Even as firemen battled flames, the cry came for action.

Police temporarily placed the blimp's pilot and Goodyear's

learned to fly under the guidance of Dutch pilot and aircraft manufacturer Anthony Fokker. In 1921, armed with her pilot's license, she returned to Chicago and ventured into stunt flying, the first licensed black pilot in the world.

Seeking funds to open a flying school for other blacks, Bessie — "Queen Bess" to her fellow stunt pilots — barnstormed the country, thrilling crowds at air shows with dangerous aerial maneuvers. In 1926, while practicing stunts for an air show for the Jacksonville, Florida, Negro Welfare League, Bessie was killed. She was brought home to Chicago and buried in Lincoln Cemetery in suburban Alsip.

Some 64 years later, the City Council of Chicago renamed Old Mannheim Road next to O'Hare

International Airport "Bessie Coleman Drive," honoring the gallant aviator who wouldn't take "no" for an answer, a pioneer in the days when aviation was struggling out of infancy.

The event that would serve as the catalyst for jump-starting commercial aviation was announced in Washington, D.C., in February 1925. Congressman Clyde Kelly of Pennsylvania sponsored legislation that influenced future commercial aviation by opening airmail routes to private entrepreneurs. The Kelly Act knocked the army, its planes, and its pilots out of their monopoly as airmail carriers.

A New Era

With aviation advancing, pilots sought more sophisticated landing places than a farmer's pasture, a racetrack, or a grass strip in Grant Park. They also needed a place to shelter, refuel, and repair their aircraft: an airport. Most major cities responded.

When the Kelly Act became law, Lambert Field in St. Louis was the best-equipped airport in the Midwest. Before the year ended, the Cleveland Airport, with 1,040 acres of land, surpassed St. Louis. Later, Ford Airport in Detroit rivaled Cleveland's facility. Meanwhile, Chicago, the nation's second-largest city, had no official airport. Something had to be done.

A string of privately owned airfields dotted the outskirts of Chicago. Checkerboard Field in west suburban Maywood served as a principal landing field for early mail flights. Ashburn Airport, at 84th and Cicero, headquarters of the local Aero Club, was another busy field.

Appalled that Chicago did not own a facility, local aviation boosters and civic leaders lobbied their aldermen for an airport. The city council, alerted to the financial rewards that might accompany airmail service, named a committee to search for a landing field and threw in a little money for the effort.

Without fanfare, the council in January 1926 authorized $25,000 for "expenses incidental to the establishment of a municipal landing field." Meanwhile, the search committee had its eye on a popular airstrip on the southwest side, 10 miles from downtown via a diagonal road known in former years as

LEFT: BESSIE COLEMAN, THE FIRST LICENSED BLACK PILOT, CIRCA 1921.
PHOTO: CHICAGO HISTORICAL SOCIETY

"the road to Widow Brown's," "Old Chicago Trail," and "Archey Road." Today its name is Archer Avenue.

The landing field at 63rd and Cicero, known as Chicago Air Park, had been attracting weekend crowds. People sat in their cars and watched aviators perform in World War I-era Jennys. The quarter-mile-square patch of land, extending four blocks north from 63rd Street and four blocks west from Cicero Avenue, was owned by the Chicago Board of Education.

Colonel Philip G. Kemp maintained a brick hangar on the property to house and repair a small stable of airplanes. He also taught flying and, on holidays and weekends, offered sightseeing excursions along the lakefront for a few dollars. A cinder runway extended from southeast to northwest. Taking off to the northwest, airplanes roared over the Laramie Golf Club.

February 26, 1926, signaled Chicago's entry into commercial aviation. The city council directed the city comptroller to execute a lease for the land at 63rd and Cicero from the Chicago Board of Education "for aviation landing purposes." A lease was negotiated at a bargain price of $1,560 a year, payable in advance.

On May 8, 1926, Chicago launched its "aviation workshop," as one writer characterized it. The airport was identified simply as a "municipal flying field," a new chapter in Chicago's development. Dignitaries saw promise in the airport and praised the new pioneers of Chicago aviation.

Marguerite Foster, the 15-year-old daughter of a member of the Association of Commerce's aviation committee, approached the Curtiss airplane, dubbed *Miss Chicago,* and smashed a bottle of "something" — the christening took place during Prohibition days — over its wheel. *Miss Chicago* later took off on its 12-hour flight to Dallas with the mail.

Among the airport supporters at the May opening was Edward J. Kelly, a city engineer and president of the South Park board. Kelly was destined to become mayor of Chicago, and years later he would play a leading role in obtaining a site for the future O'Hare International Airport.

While newspapers referred to the airport as "the new municipal flying field at 63rd and Cicero," not until more than a year later, on December 12, 1927, did Mayor William "Big Bill" Thompson officially name the field "Chicago Municipal Airport." By the end of the year, airmail contractors abandoned Checkerboard Field in Maywood and moved to the new airport. Checkerboard died a slow death and was later transformed into a forest preserve.

Only 800 arrivals and departures were logged at Municipal in 1927. Passengers were not counted, since most of the twin-cockpit planes primarily hauled airmail and air express cargo. This was also a time when pilots literally flew by the seat of their pants. Communication between aircraft and ground personnel was accomplished with little more than shouts and waves, and most operations were performed while the sun was up.

In the formative years of aviation, it was one thing to fly during daylight hours and an entirely different matter to fly at night. With only rudimentary navigational aids, night flying posed an element of risk many pilots didn't want to chance. This reluctance gradually disappeared through the efforts of the U.S. Postal Service and William P. MacCracken, Jr., a lawyer from Chicago.

When Chicago Municipal began operations, MacCracken was serving in Washington, D.C., as chief of the newly formed aeronautics branch of the Department of Commerce. He encouraged night flying, arguing that valuable hours were lost while planes sat on the ground. If pilots followed precautions, night flying was not that dangerous. The postal service took the first step when it strung out incandescent beacons every few miles along its routes to guide fliers.

At Chicago Municipal as elsewhere, night procedures were primitive at best. Pilots planning a landing after dark had to phone ahead with arrival times. Upon hearing a plane overhead, a work-

ABOVE: THE NATIONAL AIR RACES AT CURTISS FIELD, 1930. *PHOTO: CHICAGO HISTORICAL SOCIETY*

er would dash out on the field and switch on the lights. The rest was up to the pilot, perils and all.

Day and night, aviators braved hazards. The Hale Elementary School, built in 1926 near the southwest end of the field, was topped by an imposing 125-foot chimney later whittled down to a 45-foot stub. Power lines running above the Chicago Surface Line's streetcar tracks along 63rd Street and on Cicero Avenue posed another hazard to airplanes, but until buses replaced the old red "iron horses," the power lines stayed.

In 1928, its first year in business, Municipal Airport had four runways operating, each equipped with lights. A dozen hangars accommodated the growing number of planes using the field. Nearly 41,000 planes took off or landed in 1928, but only 14,000 paying passengers were aboard.

Some planes belonged to air service firms who found Municipal an excellent base for air taxi services, aviation schools, and aerial photography companies. But most of Municipal's flights hauled mail, and those planes that could carry passengers usually provided only a few seats. It was not uncommon to see more gawkers than passengers at the airport. This would

change as new planes with enclosed cabins arrived.

By 1930, airline companies, their eyes on the profits in transporting passengers, bought planes with more seats. Along with this, carriers lured the public with scheduled trips, just like the railroads. Chicago "Munie," as the airport was known, extended its main runway to 4,900 feet for the bigger and faster planes. Soon paying travelers outnumbered the gawkers.

At the end of 1930, more passengers (62,456) were recorded at Municipal than flights (58,688). Never again did the number of takeoffs and landings exceed the number of travelers. With public confidence, better planes, and

scheduled service, air travel became a reality — and with it, a need for some restrictions.

Serious Business

As Municipal Airport grew busier with commercial aviation, sightseeing and other aviation diversions were discouraged. The airport catered to the traveling public. Colonel Kemp, his flying school, and his sightseeing junkets along Lake Michigan migrated to a smaller field, as did "daredevil" air shows after a grand finale in 1933.

No longer a novelty or sideshow, aviation was coming of age. This was serious business. The city council advanced laws promoting safety in the skies. Aircraft were prohibited from trailing signs or advertising over the Loop or populated areas.

In 1931, with the number of passengers using Chicago Municipal nearing 100,000, the city constructed a modest terminal and administration building at a cost of $100,000. Improvements were installed for runways and lighting systems. These refinements, costing $774,000, were welcome projects for Chicago workers during the slim times brought on by the Great Depression.

The new terminal, which measured about half the length of a football field, was dedicated on November 15, 1931, by Mayor Anton Cermak. Major Reed Landis of the State Aeronautic Commission presented the mayor with an official airport license. Afterward, Mayor Cermak and four of his grandchildren were taken aloft for a spin in a Stinson Tri-Motor, courtesy of Century Air Lines.

BESSIE COLEMAN

NOT ONLY WAS SHE A PIONEER IN THE DAYS WHEN AVIATION WAS STRUGGLING OUT OF ITS INFANCY, BESSIE COLEMAN WAS ONE OF THE INDUSTRY'S MOST ASTOUNDING PEOPLE, BUCKING THE ODDS TO FOLLOW HER DREAM. A YOUNG BLACK MANICURIST IN CHICAGO IN 1919 WHEN THE GOODYEAR BLIMP WENT DOWN, BESSIE WAS DETERMINED TO FLY. UNABLE TO FIND A WILLING TEACHER IN AMERICA, SHE TRAVELED TO EUROPE TO STUDY UNDER ANTHONY FOKKER, BECOMING THE FIRST LICENSED BLACK PILOT IN THE WORLD. "QUEEN BESS" WAS KILLED PRACTICING STUNTS FOR AN AIR SHOW IN FLORIDA IN 1926, BUT THIS GALLANT LADY SET A STANDARD THE WORLD WILL NEVER FORGET.

Mayor Cermak was no doubt pleased that the new terminal had been completed in time for the grand opening of the 1933 World's Fair in Chicago. Unfortunately, he did not live to welcome those who flew to the city to attend it. In February 1933, he was killed in Miami by an assassin's bullet intended for President Franklin D. Roosevelt.

In the year following its dedication, the terminal opened its doors to more than 100,000 travelers. Approximately 61,000 planes arrived and departed, 11,000 fewer than the previous year. But these were bigger planes and carried more people, and in 1932 Chicago Munie captured the title of the world's busiest airport, a claim it held until the end of 1960.

The year the World's Fair opened, 1933.

more than 137,000 passengers arrived at or departed from Municipal Airport. By 1936 the number had jumped to 260,000. Much of the increase can be traced to the types of aircraft in service.

Vintage planes such as the 14-passenger Douglas DC-2, Lockheed Electra, Ford Tri-Motor, Curtiss Condor, Stinson Tri-Motor, and 10-passenger Boeing 247 carried travelers and cargo to and from Chicago. Then, in the mid-thirties, the 24-passenger Douglas DC-3 joined the competition, quickly emerging as the top choice among air carriers.

By the end of the decade the DC-3 was the mainstay of American, United, TWA, Eastern, and other airlines, carrying 95 percent of the traveling public. But more importantly, the DC-3, often hailed as the greatest airplane ever to fly, swept aviation across the threshold and into the modern age of air travel.

Chicago Municipal figured in the milestones set by the DC-3. In January 1935, a TWA DC-3 left Chicago on the first Chicago-to-New York nonstop passenger run. A month later, when American Airlines inaugurated its New York-to-Los Angeles route, its DC-3 flagship made Chicago Municipal its stopover point.

In the 1930s, the southside airport expanded its borders. Chicago Meadows Golf Club — formerly the Laramie Golf Course on the south side of 55th Street — was purchased by the city. Truck farms were next, and within a few years the airfield occupied a complete square mile, with the north boundary

extended to 55th Street and the west boundary to Central Park Avenue, exactly as they are today.

During the second half of the decade, Municipal launched major improvements to boost safety and service. With the aid of a $2 million grant from the Works Progress Administration, the airport extended, graded, and resurfaced runways and improved runway lighting systems.

At the time, the field was divided into a north and south section by the tracks of the Chicago and Western Indiana Railroad. In 1941, the tracks were rerouted north of the field. With that obstacle removed, the airport soon boasted eight sets of parallel runways.

By the end of 1941, Chicago Municipal, still the world's busiest, was averaging about 85,000 take-offs and landings a year. Aviation advisors suggested that Chicago consider adding a second airport. The attack on Pearl Harbor, how-

ever, brought more serious considerations for the city and the nation.

The War Years

Before the war, the United States was building and shipping planes through the Lend Lease program to its allies in Europe. After Pearl Harbor, production of war materiel became a full-time national labor, and cities around the country offered their services to the war effort.

In California, Douglas Aircraft Company scrapped plans to build four-engine C-54 Skymaster cargo planes in Santa Monica, fearing the possibility of a Japanese air strike. Douglas began shopping for a less vulnerable inland site. The Chicago area, with its proximity to the nation's railroads, offered several ideal locations.

Douglas Aircraft required an expansive site with enough runway space to flight-test its big cargo planes as they came off the assembly line. Chicago Municipal,

with thick cement runways that could handle the Skymasters, became one of the first locales to be considered. However, the airport was eliminated, and with good reason.

During the 1930s, the prairie land and farms that had framed the airport had become a mix of homes, apartment buildings, and industry, all nestling up to airport fences. This transformation, coupled with traffic from commercial aircraft using the field, ruled out serious consideration of Municipal.

Other places under consideration included Ford Airport in Lansing, Illinois; the Joliet and Aurora airports; Rubinkam Airport near Harvey; vacant land in Elgin and St. Charles; and a tiny village on the northwest edge of Chicago called Orchard Place.

Orchard Place was first settled by families from New England in the early 1800s. Toward the end of the century, the Wisconsin Central Railroad passed through the

settlement but, because there was no station, didn't stop there. Elvin Scott, a local orchard owner and farmer, offered part of his land for a depot if the railroad would construct one. The railroad agreed and built a depot with the name "Orchard Place" emblazoned on its side.

In the early 1920s, the dairy farms and wheat- and cornfields surrounding Orchard Place had given way to truck farms. Paved roads soon appeared, followed a short time later by the first subdivisions. This gradual urbanization contributed to the decline of the tiny community as a village. In 1936, the Orchard Place Post Office closed its doors.

In spring 1941, Edward J. Kelly was mayor of Chicago. Kelly heard that Army Air Corps General H.H. "Hap" Arnold had dispatched a committee to Chicago to recommend a site for the Douglas plant, and graciously offered the city's help. The Army Air Corps team, assisted by a panel of experts from the U.S. Army Corps of Engineers, Douglas representatives, and a group from the Chicago Association of Commerce, surveyed various sites, examining the soil, testing the wind, observing air traffic, and evaluating the available labor force. In two weeks' time, the group narrowed its selection to three sites: Lansing, Harvey, and Orchard Place.

The old political saying that it helps to have friends in high places was especially true when Orchard Place, sitting just outside Chicago's back door on the northwest side, was chosen as the site for the Douglas Aircraft plant.

Merrill C. Meigs, the former publisher of the Chicago *Herald Examiner*, had been chairman of the Chicago Aero Commission, a group that promoted aviation and advised the city on airport matters. When the war broke out, Meigs was sitting in Washington as chief of the War Production Board's Office of Airplane Production, calling the shots on such matters as new plant sites.

Meigs, like others involved in the process, was pressured for a decision on a site for the Douglas C-54 plant. The Army Air Corps wanted the factory up and running — pronto. Meigs, a Chicagoan and a friend of Mayor Kelly, was delighted the plant was coming to the Chicago

area. The mayor was happy, too. No matter where the plant was built, its presence would mean jobs for Chicago citizens. But Mayor Kelly didn't want the aircraft plant jeopardizing operations near Chicago Municipal Airport.

Finally, after much wrangling among local politicians, environmentalists, and the Army Corps of Engineers, a site was agreed upon, and in June 1942, an announcement from Meigs' office decreed that the new plant would be located at Orchard Place, based on its proximity to three railroads, the surrounding labor pool, and the city of Chicago.

The 1,400-plus acres of land were re-zoned for industrial use and

ABOVE: A TYPICAL SUNDAY AFTERNOON AT MIDWAY AIRPORT IN 1939. *PHOTO: THE JOHN CASEY COLLECTION, CHICAGO HISTORICAL SOCIETY*

the property condemned. The War Department purchased the land, and Chicago pledged to extend water lines from the city limits to the new plant.

Austin Construction Company, general contractors for the project, operating 24 hours a day, seven days a week, leveled farm buildings, orchards, and fences. Bulldozers graded fields. A command post was set up in an abandoned pickle factory, and buildings sprang up while cement was poured to lay out four runways, each 150 feet wide and more than a mile in length.

The main assembly building would require 43 acres. Since steel had "gone to war" for the produc-

tion of ships, tanks, planes, bombs, guns, and bullets, the mammoth building was constructed almost entirely of wood. It was reputed to be the largest wooden structure in the world.

Three months into the project, setup work began on a moving assembly line. Parts for the Skymasters were shipped in from other plants around the country. C-54 tails and wings arrived at Orchard Place from the Pullman Company on Chicago's southeast side.

On July 30, 1943, a little more than a year after its selection, the Orchard Place–Douglas facility was virtually complete and ready for dedication. Nearly 50,000 people watched the first Skymaster roll onto the tarmac. Christened *Miss C-54*, the plane took off on its maiden flight. Each Skymaster, once assembled, was flight-tested, delivered to the Army Air Corps people at the plant, and sent off to war.

At the dedication, General Harold George, commander of the Air Transport Command, provided uncanny foresight about future opportunities for Chicago in international travel.

"Geography smiled generously on Chicago," General George said. "For one need only study the map of the world to see that it sits at the crossroads of many of the great air routes."

From August 1943 until the end of the war, a period of two years, the Douglas plant workers produced 655 Skymaster planes for the air corps. When the fighting in Europe ended in 1945, the enemy was on the run in the South Pacific. With an allied victory in sight, war production was winding down. Defense contracts were canceled. At the Douglas–Orchard Place facility, employees pondered their fate.

Many observers believed Douglas Aircraft would convert the plant to peacetime aviation, building passenger planes. Several airlines had placed orders for commercial versions of the Skymaster, the DC-4, and the DC-6. Orchard Place, already tooled up, seemed the logical place to build them. And hadn't

there been an unofficial commitment from Douglas?

Those who attended the 1943 dedication of the Orchard Place facility remembered the words of A.E. Raymond, the vice president and director of engineering for Douglas Aircraft.

"Someday we will turn again to the days of peace," Raymond told the crowd. "Then, as now, it will be good common sense to choose Chicago, the geographical and economic center of the North American continent, as the center of production for this and other transport aircraft to follow."

After hearing those words, many thought Raymond should have a street named after him, but when VE Day arrived on September 2, 1945, Douglas Aircraft sent a different message: The company would centralize production in California. The last workers at Orchard Place were laid off. Before the end of the year, buildings and runways sat deserted.

As early as 1941, the city of Chicago had been considering a second airport. Ralph H. Burke, the city's chief engineer and a friend and confidant of Mayor Kelly, studied aviation trends and correctly predicted Chicago Municipal Airport could not, by itself, handle the expected postwar boom in aviation.

On the eve of the war in 1941, the city's Department of Aviation had been studying three recommendations for expansion: enlarging Chicago Municipal into a "super" airport; building an airport in Lake Michigan; and focusing on the northwest side of the city — ironically, in the same general area as Orchard Place.

A Global Vision

When 1944 arrived, the Chicago Planning Commission renewed the call for a second major airport, with the backing and technical expertise of eight major airlines. The consensus favored the Douglas–Orchard Place site, should it become available after the war.

At the time, Mayor Kelly was thinking about more than just a second airport. He wanted an *international* airport. In fall 1944, the mayor marched off to Washington with a delegation that included city engineer Ralph Burke; Merrill Meigs, back in the city now as chairman of the Chicago Aero Commission; Oscar Hewett, commissioner of public works; Holman Pettibone, president of the Chicago Association of Commerce; and Daniel H. Burnham, Jr., president of the Chicago Regional Planning Association and son of Chicago's

famed architect and city planner who coined the city's motto, "Make no little plans."

Kelly requested that the Civil Aeronautics Board make Chicago an international port of entry. Three airlines — American, Pan Am, and Transcontinental and Western — bolstered the mayor's case when they requested routes from Chicago to Europe and the Far East.

Eventually the city won the coveted status of port of entry, but it still lacked an airport that could measure up to international standards. Mayor Kelly went to work immediately on that project.

In 1945, the mayor approached the citizens of Chicago to gain approval for an airport expansion plan — meaning a second airport. Kelly introduced a referendum and received voter approval for a $15 million bond issue. Later in the summer, he commissioned an Airport Site Selection Committee.

"I'm not going to interfere," the mayor promised. He would keep his hands off and let the committee make the decision, but he also made it clear he wanted nothing less than "the best airport, the safest and most convenient."

The *Chicago Tribune,* which enthusiastically supported a new airport, implored the committee in an editorial to secure Douglas Airport, calling it the "best available site for additional airport facilities."

But Kelly's site selection committee would not be rushed — or pushed — into a decision. Several sites were on the agenda for appraisal, and each would be given fair consideration.

The committee examined the Clearing Industrial District off Cicero Avenue, a stone's throw south of Municipal Airport, even though Mayor Kelly didn't want anyone tampering with Municipal's future. United Airlines' president, William Patterson, also let it be known the air carriers wanted to keep Municipal. It made little sense having two airports next to each other. The committee understood the message, and the Clearing site was rejected.

Municipal itself appeared on the list, and people wondered if it wasn't just a courtesy. The airport was hemmed in by neighborhoods and major arteries. The city was not about to tear down neighborhoods.

Another site under appraisal was Lake Calumet, southeast of the city. Its drawbacks were smoke and smog from steel mills in South Chicago and Gary. (Ironically, Lake Calumet resurfaced nearly 50 years later as a possible site for a third Chicago airport, but Republicans in the state legislature blocked the proposal.)

Also resurrected was the suggestion for an airport in Lake Michigan, a concept that wouldn't go away. The idea for an airport in the lake or on the lakefront had been kicked around since 1927. This time it was dismissed as cost prohibitive.

In early discussions the committee surprisingly had spurned the

Douglas–Orchard Place airfield. Some opponents complained it was too far from downtown. Others argued that railroad tracks on the property would prohibit expansion.

And the Winner Is . . .

To the rescue came city engineer Ralph Burke. Burke overcame the objections with a plan for a 5,235-acre site that ignored the railroad tracks — for the time being. As for being too far from the Loop, the proposed Northwest Expressway (now the Kennedy Expressway) would provide a convenient connection with downtown Chicago.

Burke, with the backing of the airlines, prevailed, and Merrill Meigs and the site selection committee informed Mayor Kelly of their decision: Douglas–Orchard Place won their unanimous endorsement as the site for Chicago's super airport, if the land were available. All the city had to do was procure it.

In November 1945, Mayor Kelly was off to Washington again. Skeptics whispered the city would pay an arm and leg for the property. But Mayor Kelly succeeded in having most of the Douglas site declared war surplus property. (Some land and buildings were retained by the Air Force for military reserve and Air National

ABOVE: DANIEL H. BURNHAM, FAMED CITY PLANNER WHO COINED THE CITY'S MOTTO, "MAKE NO LITTLE PLANS." PHOTO: CHICAGO HISTORICAL SOCIETY

Guard use, a decision of some foresight in that many units stationed at the airport played a role in later domestic and international military operations, including Desert Storm in 1991 and Bosnian peacekeeping duty in 1996.)

The city council swung into action with an ordinance on November 8, 1945, "for the acquisition by the city of an airport site in Leyden and Maine townships in Cook County for the establishment of a municipal airport." The following February another ordinance authorized expenditures "for the establishment of Douglas Airport as a public airport."

On March 21, 1946, the government officially deeded 1,080 acres at the Orchard Place site to the city of Chicago. Much to the dismay — and surprise — of the naysayers, Douglas Field didn't cost the city a nickel, much less an arm and a leg.

In fall 1946, Mayor Kelly officially opened the new airport. That it had no name was the least of the airport's problems that October. There were no terminals, no passenger amenities, no control tower, no airlines, and no convenient way to get there. But Chicago already had big plans, even if it would take time to accomplish them.

Over the next several years the city acquired more than 6,000 acres of adjoining land at an average cost of about $700 an acre — a mere drop in the bucket — to expand the Douglas site into a super airport. The dream was taking shape.

In fall 1945, Mayor Kelly had been a passenger aboard American Airlines' inaugural flight from Chicago to London. Upon his return, the mayor addressed the city council and marveled at the future of air travel, envisioning a day when Chicagoans would leave their homes in the morning and "arrive in London in time for supper 10 hours later."

Kelly told the aldermen he had experienced a strange feeling, sitting in London after a 24-hour journey some 4,200 miles from Chicago. He had made the trip, he said, not only to assure people in Chicago that "air travel is safe and sure," but also to assure them that the destiny of the city was firmly linked with world airways.

"This, the greatest rail center in the world, is now in a position to become the greatest air center in the world," Kelly said. "This is our opportunity. This is our destiny. We must seize it."

And seize it Chicago did.

Chapter Two

'Make No Little Plans'

ity fathers who jour-
neyed to the Douglas
property were awed at
the deserted airfield and
empty hangars. One might speculate
they heard a voice challenging them:
"Here it is. What will you do with it?"

There is an old maxim authored
by Daniel Hudson Burnham, the
legendary city planner and architect, whose words around the turn
of the century were immortalized
for future Chicago generations:
"Make no little plans; they have no
magic to stir men's blood and probably will not be realized."

In 1946, when the city awakened
as owner of an abandoned airfield,
Burnham's words provided inspira-
tion, if not direction. Kelly's "super
airport" would involve more than
patching over Douglas Field, constructing access roads and terminals. This sleeping giant would
stretch beyond the cornfields and
farms. Land had to be annexed or
purchased, soil tested.

First, Ralph Burke, the former
city engineer, was hired as a consultant to draw up a master plan.
Burke, an MIT graduate, had worn
many hats as a city engineer. A jack
of all trades, he moved from
department to department helping
lay out streets and highways for the

city and designing a mass transit
subway system beneath the Loop.

The airport project would be
monumental. Burke sat at the drawing board estimating land requirements, designing basic plans for
terminals and runways, and setting
a timetable for each construction
phase. He calculated costs and
helped secure money from federal,
state, and city sources.

While Burke's blueprints took
shape, the airport made its debut
on October 3, 1946. With Mayor
Kelly presiding, the "barebones"
airport welcomed its first commercial flight, a cargo plane.

The city approved Burke's
master plan in early 1947, and the
following year federal and state
agencies gave their blessing. All
that was lacking was funding.

In spring 1947, Democratic party
bosses dumped Ed Kelly and elected businessman Martin Kennelly
mayor. Kennelly supported the airport — to a degree. The facility
would not come cheap, and thus
far the city had received only

LEFT: MAYOR MARTIN KENNELLY SENDS
THE CHICAGO FLAG ON A PAN AM ROUND-
THE-WORLD FLIGHT FROM MUNICIPAL
AIRPORT JUNE 30, 1947. *PHOTO: CHICAGO
HISTORICAL SOCIETY*

modest help from the federal government and the legislature.

The Bottom Line

Chicago Municipal, the world's busiest airfield in 1947, had been losing money since 1939 at the rate of nearly $80,000 a year. Mayor Kennelly insisted that the city not bear the entire burden of building a new airport. He halted construction until the airlines agreed to pay their share of the bill.

At the time, the nation's domestic airlines were not exactly rolling in money. The long-awaited postwar travel boom had never materialized. Carriers, burdened by purchases of new and bigger airplanes, were operating in the red. Kennelly was not swayed.

According to the *Chicago Tribune,* after meeting with the mayor the airlines created the Chicago Airlines Top Committee consisting of representatives of the domestic carriers. The Top Committee would adopt policies for air operations in the city and negotiate landing fees at the new airport. More important at this phase, the airlines pledged to contribute $60,000 annually toward construction. Kennelly gave the order to resume work.

There remained the matter of a name. Initially, the new venture was known as Douglas Airfield, but in official proceedings the airport was called Chicago Orchard Airfield. Thus tags on luggage bound for the airport were inscribed with the letters ORD (as they are today), an abbreviation for Orchard.

Neither the Douglas nor Orchard names caused much excitement in a

city that enthusiastically named streets, parks, and museums after its heroes. Clearly, a more fitting and imaginative name had to be found.

The city didn't have to look far. America, still aglow over victory in World War II, had no shortage of heroes, and in Chicago the name of a former resident, navy air hero Butch O'Hare, was already famous.

O'Hare — the Legend

O'Hare was born in Missouri, but he had a Chicago connection. He had lived in Chicago with his father before the war, and father and son had owned property in the city.

Alderman John Hoellen launched the campaign to name the airport after Butch O'Hare.

"The naval air cadets [at Glenview Naval Air Station] and Lieutenant Commander Olson proposed O'Hare's name, and they turned to me for help in the council," Hoellen says.

The alderman found a powerful ally in Colonel Robert R. McCormick, the outspoken publisher of the *Chicago Tribune* and a decorated veteran of World War I. McCormick endorsed the O'Hare name and bolstered the campaign with editorials and street polls.

O'Hare (nicknamed "Butch" by his sister) was born March 13, 1914, in St. Louis. He was a tall, good-natured honor student at Western Military Academy in Alton, Illinois.

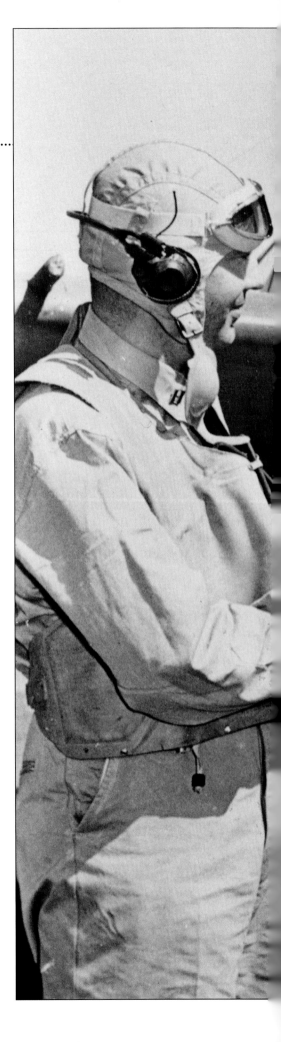

Since childhood, he had dreamed of attending the Naval Academy. In 1933, he was accepted at Annapolis and graduated four years later. After a duty tour aboard a destroyer, the young ensign made up his mind to be a navy pilot.

O'Hare enrolled in flight training at Pensacola Naval Air Station in Florida. After winning his pilot's wings, he and his bride, Rita, left for his next station in California.

On December 7, 1941, the Japanese attack on Pearl Harbor plunged America into war. One day later, O'Hare was on his way to the South Pacific, joining the carrier U.S.S. *Lexington*. In less than two months, he received his first taste of combat in an air battle that was to engrave his name in naval history.

The *Lexington* had been ordered to find and destroy the Japanese fleet. As it steamed toward the enemy base at Rabaul on New Britain Island in the South Pacific, enemy scout planes spotted the ship. Japanese bombers were quickly dispatched to sink the American carrier.

The first wave of planes encountered fighters from the *Lexington* and were destroyed. The Americans returned to the carrier to refuel and rearm their planes, unaware that while they rested on the carrier deck, a second squadron of Japanese planes was approaching.

Butch O'Hare and his wingman, patrolling in Grumman F4F Wildcats, sighted nine enemy bombers heading for a second attempt on the *Lexington*. The two pilots became the sole protectors of the carrier and its 3,000 men.

O'Hare and his wingman attacked the bombers, flying into a hail of cannon and machine gun fire. As the two Americans opened fire, the guns on the wingman's plane jammed, leaving Butch in his Grumman Wildcat to prevent the Japanese assault single-handedly.

With his 50-caliber machine guns blazing, O'Hare knocked out two bombers. In a second run, he sent three more enemy planes spinning to the sea in flames. In a third encounter, O'Hare crippled a sixth bomber just as fighter planes arrived from the *Lexington* and finished off the attackers.

O'Hare was credited with saving the *Lexington*. Two months later he was summoned to the White House, where President Franklin D. Roosevelt presented him with the Congressional Medal of Honor, the nation's highest award. The president described O'Hare's bravery as one of the most daring, if not the most daring, single actions in the history of combat aviation.

O'Hare returned to the Pacific to train pilots for night combat. Eighteen months later, on patrol from the U.S.S. *Enterprise* off Tarawa in the Gilbert Islands, O'Hare's group engaged a party of Japanese fighter planes. During the battle, a navy pilot saw O'Hare's plane leave the formation and disappear in the darkness. O'Hare was never seen again. Six years later, his name was permanently inscribed on the world's busiest airport.

During a city council proceeding, Butch O'Hare was referred to as "a Chicago boy." Actually, he first set foot in Chicago after the divorce of his parents, Selma and Edward O'Hare. Butch's father, a St. Louis attorney, pulled up stakes after the divorce and moved to Chicago, where he unwittingly earned a place for himself in the annals of Chicago's gangland lore.

Good Intentions, But ...

In St. Louis, Edward H. O'Hare, Sr., had represented the inventor of the mechanical rabbit used at dog racing tracks. Through this association, O'Hare became quite wealthy. When his client unexpectedly died, he plunged into racing on his own.

Alderman Edward Burke, chairmen of the city council finance committee and a history buff, has researched the senior O'Hare's days in Chicago.

According to Burke, the elder O'Hare operated a kennel club that he later merged with one owned by Chicago's premier gangster, Al Capone. While O'Hare abhorred gangsters, he believed he could work with Capone and still keep his distance from the mob. Above all, he didn't want his association with gangsters to spoil his son's chances of attending the naval academy.

In 1928, the government dispatched Special Agent Frank Wilson of the Treasury Department to Chicago to pursue Capone on tax

evasion charges. Wilson succeeded in planting two informants in Capone's organization. A big break came when one of them alerted Wilson to an incriminating document in a police file cabinet: a handwritten ledger listing illegal and undeclared Capone profits of more than half a million dollars from gambling.

When Capone heard that Wilson was closing in, he ordered the

agent's murder, but Wilson's informants warned him, and the agent and his wife fled their room in the Sheridan Plaza Hotel, narrowly missing their planned execution in the hotel garage.

Based on evidence Wilson collected, Capone was indicted for evading taxes. Two weeks before the trial in 1931, another "mystery" informant met Wilson on a deserted Chicago street corner. The informant passed some startling information: Capone had fixed the jury selected for his upcoming trial! Wilson immediately contacted presiding Judge James H. Wilkerson.

The morning the trial opened, Judge Wilkerson stunned Capone by

replacing the "fixed" jury panel with a panel from another courtroom. The new jurors found Capone guilty of income tax evasion, and Scarface Al was sentenced to 11 years in prison. The mobster's business partner, Edward H. O'Hare, Sr., assumed control of Sportsman's Park and Hawthorne Racetrack and prospered over the years. The tale, however, doesn't end there.

On November 8, 1939, a week before Capone was released from prison suffering from neurosyphilis, O'Hare was driving home from Sportsman's Park and noticed a car following him. He pressed the gas pedal to the floor, but his pursuers

caught up with him at Ogden and Rockwell on Chicago's near southwest side. One of the car's passengers fired two blasts from a shotgun, killing the track owner, whose car then leaped a curb and plowed into a trolley pole. Capone's boys had given Al his "coming home" present.

The murder, Alderman Burke says, was never solved, but the untold story of the elder O'Hare's relationship with the Chicago mob was revealed in 1949, the year his son's name was under consideration for the new airport.

In a 1949 *Colliers* magazine article, Agent Frank Wilson, who

went on to head the Secret Service, disclosed the identity of one of his most important informants in the Capone case: Edward H. O'Hare, Sr.

Wilson related that the elder O'Hare, hoping to smooth things for his son's entry into Annapolis, had approached the government and offered his services to help snare Capone. Over time, O'Hare passed along valuable information. One item proved to be the most important factor in convicting Capone.

Agent Wilson disclosed that it was Edward O'Hare who met him on that deserted street corner in 1931 and told him Capone had

"fixed" the jury. When Wilson doubted his story, O'Hare had shoved a list with the names of the tainted jurors at him. At the time, not even Judge Wilkerson had the jury list. Had O'Hare not alerted Wilson about the jury tampering, Al Capone would have walked out of court a free man. Instead, he spent years in the federal prison system, the last five in humiliation on Alcatraz Island fending off fellow cons.

Agent Wilson praised O'Hare as "the most important single factor" in nabbing Capone. Years after his violent death, Edward H. O'Hare, Sr., was exonerated, at least in some measure, and his son, Butch, had not been tarnished. He had attained and even surpassed his dream of becoming a naval officer — and more.

The proposed ordinance to name the airport "O'Hare Field, Chicago International Airport" was read to the city council on June 22, 1949, with the backing of Alderman Hoellen, the city's newspapers, veterans' groups, the Navy Air Men of America, and the Navy League.

Alderman Theron Merryman moved to concur that "this great airfield" be named in memory of Lieutenant Commander Edward H. O'Hare, who alone on February 20, 1943, heroically "saved the carrier *Lexington* when it stood as a thin line of defense between the attacking enemy and our shores." The ordinance passed, 43-1.

Credit Where It's Due

A second ordinance renamed another Chicago airport for a city aviation pioneer. In 1949, Chicago operated three airports: Douglas–Orchard Field, Chicago Municipal, and a newcomer on an island off Grant Park in Lake Michigan.

Northerly Island, a man-made island south of Chicago's Loop at 14th Street, was one of a string of five islands with gardens and parks proposed for the Chicago World's Fair of 1933. Because money was short during the Great Depression, only one island was built, the one farthest north.

When Congress enacted a federal grant program in 1946 for new airport construction, Merrill C. Meigs and the Chicago Aero Commission saw an opportunity for an airport on Northerly Island, less than 10 minutes from downtown Chicago. The day the grants were handed out in Washington, Chicago was first in line.

Northerly Island was leased from the Chicago Park District and construction began in 1947. The following year, with a single runway extending north and south, the airport was ready to handle traffic.

On December 10, 1948, Mayor Martin Kennelly presided over the ribbon-cutting ceremony. A plane flew over the harbor and dropped 51 glass bottles, each bearing a gift certificate ranging from $5 to $100 "good at any State Street store." Seventy-five members of the Flying Farmers club flew in with their families for the festivities. Landing fees for the day were $1.

A *Chicago Tribune* editorial expressed "great satisfaction" with Northerly Field, calling it "the most convenient airport of any large city in the world." (The paper also praised the city for pushing the development of Douglas Airport, destined to be the world's largest.)

The $2 million landing strip on Northerly Island was an immediate hit with private pilots, business fliers, and commuter airlines. In its resolution on June 22, 1949, the council named the airport Meigs Field, honoring aviation pioneer Merrill C. Meigs. Meigs had served Chicago's interests in landing the Douglas Aircraft plant and played a key role in the plant's selection as the site for Chicago's third airport. (Ironically, two years before the O'Hare name was chosen for Douglas Field, navy groups and the American Legion had suggested naming the lakefront field "O'Hare Airport.")

Chicago Municipal Airport also received a new name that year. In a letter dated October 6, the Chicago Aero Commission recommended that the southwestside field be known as "Chicago Midway Airport."

On December 12, the following ordinance was adopted: "Inasmuch as Chicago is now the hub of air transport and air commerce, a more descriptive name is suggested," the ordinance declared. "Hence, it is the sense of the city council that this airport be designated as Chicago Midway Airport, in keeping with our geographical position as the leader in transportation."

Alderman Merryman had also submitted an aviation committee report that the new name would commemorate the heroes of the Battle of Midway Island in the Pacific where, during two days in January 1942, U.S. planes sank two Japanese carriers and permanently crippled the enemy fleet.

So ended the naming and renaming of Chicago's airports. There is one footnote, however: In December 1958, the council modified the name "O'Hare Field, Chicago International Airport" to "Chicago O'Hare International Airport."

Another ceremony, this one to anoint the airport with O'Hare's name, took place on September 19, 1949, with Butch O'Hare's mother as guest of honor. The stands were packed with gold brass, including Rear Admiral Dan Gallery, a Chicagoan who captured the U-505 German submarine during the war.

Public Works Commissioner Oscar Hewitt described the program as "a spectacle to do honor to a Chicago boy, an affair as he would have wished if he were here." Later, as Mrs. O'Hare unveiled a plaque honoring her son, a flight of Navy Banshee jets swooped across the field.

ABOVE: 1949 HOLIDAY TRAVELERS CROWD THE UNITED AIRLINES TERMINAL AT CHICAGO MUNICIPAL (MIDWAY) AIRPORT.
PHOTO: CHICAGO HISTORICAL SOCIETY

Gaining Ground

Now that it had a name, O'Hare continued the business of becoming an airport — and if it were to be a major airport, O'Hare needed more space. The Douglas runways measured only 5,000 to 5,500 feet, hardly long enough to accommodate the

BUTCH O'HARE

COMDR. CHUCK BRANS-FIELD OF CHICAGO, A DECORATED NAVY FLIER IN WORLD WAR II, WAS SHOT DOWN OFF TARAWA AND TAKEN PRISONER. HE TRAINED WITH BUTCH O'HARE IN PENSACOLA. "WE ALL KNEW HIM AS ONE OF THE FINER PEO-PLE, THE BEST THE REG-ULAR NAVY HAD. THAT 'HERO' CRAP IS FUNNY, BUT IN BUTCH'S CASE IT WAS TRUE. IF YOU HAD HIM ON YOUR WING OR YOU WERE ON HIS WING, YOU COULD DEPEND ON HIM. THAT WAS THE LITMUS TEST YOU JUDGED EVERYONE ON.

"AS FOR NAMING THE AIRPORT FOR BUTCH, IF ANYBODY DESERVED IT, HE DID. BUTCH WAS THE REAL THING, ONE OF NATURE'S TRUE GENTLE-MEN, ALMOST A SAINT. HIS FATHER DIED FOR BUTCH AND BUTCH DIED FOR HIS COUNTRY. HOW MUCH FURTHER CAN YOU GO FROM THAT?"

four-engine jets soon to be rolling out of aircraft plants. To make room, two railroads on the west side of the airport agreed to pull up their tracks and relocate them.

In all, about 7,000 acres of prop-erty were acquired. The city wisely hired local real estate appraisers to negotiate sales. More than 4,000 parcels, most of them farms, were purchased initially, at an average price of about $700 an acre.

Many farm homes were demol-ished after being sold, but some owners elected to cart their houses on flatbed trailers to new locations. One of the most unusual moves from the airport land involved a church.

St. John's Evangelical & Reformed Church was built almost a century before the airport and served the rural community's early German immi-grants. When the airport came along, parishioners decided to move the old building to nearby Bensenville.

"It was our church," says retired farmer Harold Schultz. "Everybody just decided we should preserve it."

Moving the church, whose spire stood some 90 feet high, proved a massive undertaking. Just before Christmas 1951, the building was raised up and placed on dollies supported by 32 B-17 bomber tires. The relocation didn't begin for two months, and during the interval parishioners parked cars beneath the church while attending services above. In February 1952, the journey began.

"It was moved down the main roads during the day," Schultz says of the three-mile trip. "Traffic wasn't like it is today, but they had to lower electric wires and things like that."

At one point where a road banked, the church tilted precariously. Schultz remembers some anxious moments when the tires on that side suddenly began blowing out. But St. John's — now called St. John's United Church of Christ — arrived intact at Foster Avenue and Route 83 in Bensenville.

One part of St. John's heritage was left behind: its cemetery. Three cemeteries once occupied airport land. One was relocated, but St. John's and Rest Haven remain because of difficulty in locating relatives for permission to dig up and move graves.

Today, passengers glancing out their windows might be startled by the two fenced-in cemeteries along one runway, colorful flowers adorning the graves. But that isn't the only curiosity travelers might see.

In building new runways and extending others, engineers discovered ground areas containing soil too soft and flexible to support runways that would handle heavier planes.

The problem was quickly solved. On the south side of the airfield, a plot of heavier soil was found, dug up, and hauled across the field to replace the soft spots for the new runways, leaving behind a 94-acre pit. Thus was born Lake O'Hare.

If O'Hare called itself an airport in its early days, its operations did little to confirm it. At the end of 1949, only 259,000 passengers used the field, while Midway counted more than 3 million. Where was everyone?

During O'Hare's construction phase, airlines were in no hurry to move in. For one thing, carriers were reluctant to share the field with the military, which had retained about 300 acres of the land.

In June 1950, when Korean troops invaded South Korea, President Truman responded with military force. Air Force fighter pilots, many

from the O'Hare base, soon found themselves flying combat missions in the Far East. As the war progressed, more pilots arrived at O'Hare for flight training, fueling rumors that the Air Force had designs on the field. Nothing came of the rumors.

Years earlier, the Air Force had promised to remove active units from the field by 1952, leaving only a reserve base. When 1952 rolled around, the Air Force, like an unwanted relative, was still hanging around. The situation grew worse when an Air Force plan for an ammunition dump on the field was revealed. The airlines were livid: They would not subject passengers to the hazards of landing next to an ammunition dump.

From the beginning, the city and the airlines also worried about civilian jetliners and military planes

Chapter Three

Catalyst for Growth

··

Among the American public, there was no doubt that flying had become the "preferred means" of travel, the most sensible choice to go from one place to another, quickly and safely. A glance at the amount of passenger traffic filing through Chicago's three airports verified the growth and popularity of air travel. In just eight years, the number of people using the city's airports had risen by 7.5 million people. Traffic at O'Hare International Airport, the city's flagship facility, had risen from 259,000 passengers in 1949, the year it opened, to more than a million in 1957. The days of the white-knuckled air traveler had all but disappeared.

Six years before President Kennedy dedicated O'Hare in 1963, a little-known turning point in the development of the airport was reached, one that would have a profound effect on its future. City architects — the architectural firm of Naess-Murphy, and Landrum & Brown of Cincinnati (one of the nation's top airport consulting firms) — had projected the airport's future needs and concluded that the late Ralph Burke's master plan, drawn years earlier, fell short of meeting requirements of the advancing jet age. Burke's blue-print, like the proverbial super-highway that becomes obsolete before it is finished, was in need of drastic revision.

With 17 scheduled airlines using the airport at the beginning of 1957, O'Hare was recognized as a major destination and transfer point. United Airlines claimed O'Hare as its hub, and American Airlines considered the airport one of its major bases. The city quickly realized that these giant carriers would soon be bringing new and bigger planes to the airport. With construction underway for the Northwest Expressway (Kennedy Expressway) linking the airport with the Loop (Chicago's downtown), Mayor Richard J. Daley retained Naess-Murphy (later C.F. Murphy & Associates, then Murphy/Jahn) for the design and building of two domestic terminals, the existing ones having been found to be inadequate and too small.

Neither were manufacturers blind to the number of people flying. Long-range jetliners, already on order from the world's air

carriers, included Boeing's 707, which carried twice as many passengers as its predecessors. These planes would present new demands on airports for space, inside and outside the terminals.

The big planes, with broader wingspans, required more maneuvering room around arrival and departure gates. Inside the terminal, additional space was needed to accommodate more passengers. It also followed that more passengers meant more automobile, bus, and taxi traffic around the terminals, as well as more space for parking cars.

With input from the airlines, O'Hare's architects began their revisions and produced a new plan, one far different from Burke's pentagonal design. The new version provided for an orderly, compact arrangement of terminals and approach roads.

By February 1958, one year before jets came into service at O'Hare, a critical decision had been reached for a revamped design for the airport, the cost of the first phase of development to be financed by revenue bonds of $120 million and underwritten by the airlines. These improvements included the longer runways needed by jet aircraft and a rearrangement of the terminal complex. The 1958 plan created a horseshoe-shaped configuration of two huge, tinted-glass domestic terminal buildings, connected to each other and anchored by a modern rotunda-like restaurant tower designed by architect Gertrude Kerbis. A third building was modeled as an international terminal. Each of the rectangular buildings measured more than 750 feet in length. Extending out from each terminal were long Y-shaped fingers, with departure and arrival gates located along the concourses.

Adjacent to the terminals was a two-level approach road system, designed to prevent congestion between departing and arriving ground traffic, With input from consultant/architects Nick Le Bar and Alfred Benesch Associates, the two-level approach road system — the same one air travelers see today — established a smooth flow of ground traffic in and out of the airport.

Cars, buses, and taxicabs carrying departing passengers were directed to the upper level, where skycaps waited at curbside to check luggage.

ABOVE: AN AVALANCHE OF BAGGAGE HITS O'HARE DURING THE 1978 HOLIDAY SEASON. *PHOTO: CHICAGO HISTORICAL SOCIETY.* RIGHT: A CENTRAL DESTINATION AND DEPARTURE POINT FOR BOTH INTERNATIONAL AND DOMESTIC AIRLINES, O'HARE IS UNITED AIRLINES' HUB. *PHOTO BY GARY CONNER©/INDEX STOCK*

Or a passenger could simply enter the terminal, and walk a few steps to ticket counters, or proceed to the boarding areas.

Arriving passengers disembarked on the upper level, walked through the concourse to the terminal building, and boarded an escalator down to the lower level, where they retrieved luggage from baggage carousels. Outside the baggage claim area, cars, limousines, buses, and taxicabs waited to transport the arriving passengers to destinations in the city and suburbs.

The city and its architects realized they had made a wise decision in rethinking Ralph Burke's airport design plan, for in that year — with Midway Airport nearly a ghost field — O'Hare recorded over 16 million passengers, 15 million more than had used the new airport six years earlier! Had the city not taken a second look at the airport design as it stood in 1957, it is conceivable that a major and costly renovation of O'Hare would have been necessary.

This, then, was the airport President Kennedy dedicated in 1963: a 7,000-acre facility with two modern terminals (which won C.F. Murphy & Associates a prestigious award from the American Institute of Architects), an enlarged and newly refurbished international terminal building, 500 acres of hangar area, a two-level system for arrivals and departures that created a systematic flow of people and traffic to and from the centralized group of terminals, a telephone exchange, and a post office.

Air Travel Mecca

O'Hare, now the world's busiest airport, would continue its growth as a mecca for domestic and international air travelers. Airport planners, perhaps mindful of the city's motto "Make no little plans," had also allowed for future expansion, and it came sooner than expected.

In 1968, O'Hare's traffic was growing at a rate of 3 million passengers a year. Arrivals and departures had nearly doubled to 30 million passengers in five years, bringing congestion and flight delays. And ahead loomed the arrival of a new generation of planes from aircraft manufacturers. The rapidly changing aviation industry was about to cross still another threshold. At aircraft plants around the nation, assembly lines were being tooled for

LEFT: MORE THAN 184,000 PASSENGERS GO THROUGH O'HARE'S TERMINALS DAILY. *PHOTO BY PAUL MERIDETH© /TONY STONE WORLDWIDE*

planes such as Lockheed's 1011 Tristar, the Douglas DC-10, and the largest of them all, Boeing's 747, capable of seating 366 or more passengers, nearly three times the passenger load of the 707. The new models would have a significant effect on the world's airports.

Passengers noticed few, if any, major inconveniences while the city reshaped, extended, and widened concourses for the big planes, adding more gates and more room for passengers. Of course, expansion brought a few negative comments from the public. Most complaints focused on walking distances from terminals to loading gates, or from

ABOVE: A GENIAL AIRPORT POLICE OFFICER ASSISTS YOUNG PASSENGERS AT SECURITY-CONSCIOUS O'HARE. *PHOTO BY PETER J. SCHULZ, CITY OF CHICAGO, DEPT. OF AVIATION*

parking facilities to terminals, familiar grievances to large airports. The Chicago *Daily News* added its two cents in 1966 with an editorial complaining about "too much walking," which carried the headline, "O'Hare: No Place for Corns."

To ease the hike through pedestrian thoroughfares, the city installed moving sidewalks. Years later, when United Airlines built a new terminal,

moving sidewalks were introduced in the B and C concourses. By 1993, when International Terminal 5 made its debut, moving sidewalks had become standard equipment.

O'Hare's First Skyscraper

Beyond O'Hare's terminals, another new building appeared in 1973, the first and only "skyscraper" at the airport. The O'Hare Hilton, a 10-story luxury hotel designed by Carter Manny, Jr., and John M. Novack of C.F. Murphy & Associates, mirrored the tinted-glass styling of the terminals. With the addition of the Hilton, O'Hare

became an airport where passengers could step off a plane and walk to a hotel lobby.

Over the years, the O'Hare Hilton has acquired an international reputation for quality. Since its 1962 renovation, the hotel now boasts 858 guest rooms, 42 meeting rooms, 9 banquet rooms, 3 ballrooms, and an indoor pool, health club, steam room, and golf simulator.

In hotel corridors, corporate giants from around the world mingle with everyday tourists and that army of hardy business fliers, the "road warriors," while conducting meetings or just relaxing. Guests may find themselves rubbing elbows with czars and stars from major league baseball, the National Football League, or the National Basketball Association. On the corporate level, a partial roster of clients includes the Ford Motor Company, Arthur Andersen, Mitsubishi International, the American Medical Association, and the American Automobile Association (AAA). Even the names of Elton John and the Dalai Lama have found their way into the hotel's guest register.

O'Hare International's strategic location generated a building boom in surrounding areas. Other fine hotels and motels sprang up to serve O'Hare's travelers, not only with superior accommodations but with meeting rooms, exercise facilities, and more. Most of these outlying hotels furnish courtesy vans to transport guests to and from airport terminals in a few minutes' time.

In downtown Chicago, about a half-hour away, a new generation of hotels has joined the established

ABOVE: JETS WAIT TO TAKE OFF FROM O'HARE INTERNATIONAL. *PHOTO BY PETER J. SCHULZ, CITY OF CHICAGO, DEPT. OF AVIATION*

roster of traditional hotels, welcoming tourists, business travelers, and the city's booming convention trade.

City Within a City

While not on a par with the Taj Mahal, O'Hare resembles a massive yet friendly metropolis. It has been called, and rightly so, a city within a city, a beehive of activity, with employees on a common mission. Each day, people who work at the airport assist the "temporary" citizens by providing the same services, comforts, and safety they would expect at home. Need a doctor? O'Hare boasts a full-service health care facility, staffed by doctors and nurses from the University of Illinois at Chicago Medical Center. And should an unexpected toothache threaten to spoil a trip, this airport has a dental facility where two dentists are waiting with state-of-the-art equipment.

For elderly travelers or those who cannot walk, the city provides free wheelchairs and motorized carts. The Travelers & Immigrants Aid office extends information, directions, and assistance. A USO lounge for servicemen and servicewomen offers refreshments and information. Want to change money? Two banks in the International Terminal convert foreign currency.

O'Hare obliges its patrons with restaurants and sports bars, cafeterias and snack bars, and lounge seating. Visitors can browse through shops that range from chic women's boutiques to fashionable men's stores, and discover gifts and goods of all varieties, from gourmet coffee to greeting cards and aviation memorabilia.

RIGHT: JUSTLY TERMED A CITY WITHIN A CITY, O'HARE OFFERS NUMEROUS PASSENGER CONVENIENCES. HERE, TRAVELERS ENJOY A QUICK BITE AT O'HARE'S MIDWEST MARKET. *PHOTO BY PETER J. SCHULZ, CITY OF CHICAGO, DEPT. OF AVIATION*

On the mezzanine level in Terminal 2, a chapel is staffed by a full-time chaplain. Supported by major faiths, the Airport Chapel celebrated its 35th anniversary in November 1995; the late Joseph Cardinal Bernardin represented the Chicago Archdiocese.

No airport is immune to flight cancellations or delays caused by adverse weather. When these conditions occur, hotel space in the area is sometimes at a premium. In the blizzard that paralyzed the East Coast in January 1966, O'Hare became a temporary home for more than 1,000 passengers whose destinations were snowed in and shut down. Airport personnel swung into action with Chicago's unique Passenger Assistance Program, supplying stranded travelers with cots, blankets, pillows,

refreshments, and travel kits, all without charge.

One passenger from New Jersey wrote the city that his family's visit would never be forgotten. "Everyone we met [at the airport] was wonderful to us and went out of his way to make a bad situation bearable. In fact, we really had a good time."

"We're very proud of this program," said Mayor Richard M. Daley, the current chief executive and son of the former mayor. "It sets Chicago apart as being the friendliest city in the world."

Mother Nature struck again in February 1995 with another eastern storm that grounded flights. Again the airport spread out the welcome mat for stranded passengers. Many of O'Hare's "temporary" citizens boarded "El" trains to the Loop or to sample Chicago attractions.

Almost half the people using O'Hare are business travelers, and facilities for doing business right at the airport are available. American

Airlines offers its Executive Center, a state-of-the-art complex with 19 conference rooms. The center provides electronic and audiovisual equipment, fax machines, flip charts, and copiers — even a catering service. The Skybird Meeting Center in the Rotunda between terminals 2 and 3 also has meeting rooms available and provides catering services.

O'Hare the Beautiful

To keep this "city within a city" beautiful, street sweepers make their appointed rounds on the roadways and walkways, inside and outside the terminals, at all hours of the day and night. Public rest rooms are cleaned and monitored around the clock. Landscaping adds an unexpected splash of color to the airport. More than 1,200 trees were planted

along the terminals and approach roads in 1993 and 1994. Each spring, flower beds and planters around the terminals dazzle visitors with daffodils, daylilies, roses, geraniums, impatiens, and tulips.

O'Hare maintains its own police force and fire department. Three fire rescue units are stationed at the field, serving not only the airport but the hotel and parking areas. Fire Station 3, completed in September 1994, serves as an air rescue unit and training center.

Like many travelers, O'Hare's patrons need a place to put their automobiles. In 1973, the city completed a six-level parking facility directly behind the O'Hare Hilton Hotel. At the time of its opening, parking area A was reputed to be the largest "garage" building in the world, accommodating 9,300 cars. Since then, O'Hare's parking capability has more than doubled.

By 1995, O'Hare offered a total of six parking areas, four for short-term parking and two outlying lots for

long-term parking. The lots are served by shuttle buses and the Airport Transit System (ATS). The six parking lots accommodate more than 18,000 cars.

The airport's well-lighted parking lots reflect a concern for security and assistance, top priorities at airports everywhere. Call boxes are strategically located in every parking area, should a motorist need help with a dead battery, lost keys, or even finding his or her car. Attendants in courtesy vans assist people with these and other problems at no charge.

In parking building A, the city has capitalized on its reputation as a sports mecca, adopting a sports theme at elevator stations on all six floors of the building to help remind motorists where they parked. Each floor carries a sports insignia — White Sox, Cubs, Bears, Bulls, Blackhawks, or World Cup — and a speaker system plays a sound track identified with that particular sport.

In 1993 the city privatized its parking operations, selecting Standard Parking to run day-to-day operations. In 1994, in an effort to boost minority- and women-owned business participation in subcontracts, Chicago awarded eight such firms contracts for maintenance operations in its airport parking system.

In the terminals, automobile rental agencies extend their services to arriving passengers. Travelers who continue their journeys by car find that O'Hare is a convenient departure point, not only to Chicago, but to the Midwest as well. Chicago's Loop is about a 25-minute drive via the Kennedy Expressway. A network of major highways and expressways

rings the airport, providing convenient access to cities inside and outside the metropolitan area. From O'Hare, for example, the drive to Rockford, Illinois's third-largest city, is roughly 50 minutes. Surrounding states such as Indiana and Wisconsin are easily accessible, thanks to interstate highways.

While all roads seemingly lead to and from O'Hare, not all are paved

with concrete or asphalt. Because of Mayor Richard J. Daley's foresight during the 1950s planning phase of the Northwest Expressway, Chicago's modern CTA rapid transit trains whiz alongside automobiles on the Kennedy Expressway, carrying passengers and airport workers from Chicago's Loop and other parts of the city to the airport at the bargain price of $1.50. The 40-minute

ABOVE: THE BLIZZARD OF JANUARY 1966 BROUGHT FLIGHTS AT O'HARE TO A STANDSTILL. *PHOTO: THE NEAL CALLAHN COLLECTION, CHICAGO HISTORICAL SOCIETY.* OPPOSITE: CHICAGO'S AIRPORT TRANSIT SYSTEM CONNECTS O'HARE WITH THE DOWNTOWN LOOP. *PHOTO BY PETER J. SCHULZ, CITY OF CHICAGO, DEPT. OF AVIATION*

journey from the Loop to the airport, with stops along the way, terminates beneath the airport's main parking lot in a clean, quiet station reminiscent of some of London's better tube stations. This "El" stop is deserving of the architectural award that it received. Its glass-block walls, extending the length of the station platform on both sides, are backlit with gold illumination and suggest a definite feeling of luxury. Commuters arriving on El trains board escalators that take them to a pedestrian thoroughfare, which then connects with domestic terminals.

If there was a blemish on O'Hare's reputation, it lay in the original international terminal. In its early days the terminal was adequate, but as jumbo jets opened the world to more travelers, it was overwhelmed by the traffic. Congestion became worse, especially when more than one of the big planes arrived at the same time. Adding to the situation were long lines at customs and immigration gates. Returning from Rome, the late television commentator Len O'Connor looked at the horde of angry passengers and dryly remarked, "It reminds me of those old ·movies of immigrants arriving at Ellis Island."

City planners agreed; the outmoded international terminal had seen its day. A new "jet age" terminal was needed. In the meantime, the old terminal was unceremoniously moved to the ground level of the enclosed parking building. On the original terminal's site, United Airlines began erecting a "state-of-the-art" replacement designed by Helmut Jahn of Murphy/Jahn. Finally, in 1993, a sleek new $618 million international terminal made its debut as Terminal 5, a short distance from the domestic aviation center.

"Cargo City"

As O'Hare's complexion changed with the construction of the United and International terminals, another development had been taking place across the field. With the jet age spreading its wings, American business was introduced to the advantages of shipping goods by air. Cargo holds of jetliners, or the entire body of a jet freighter, offered a fast

CAMP O'HARE

WHEN ADVERSE WEATHER CAUSES FLIGHT CANCELLATIONS, HOTEL SPACE IN THE AREA IS SOMETIMES AT A PREMIUM. DURING THE JANUARY 1966 BLIZZARD THAT PARALYZED THE EAST COAST, O'HARE AIRPORT BECAME A TEMPORARY HOME FOR MORE THAN 1,000 PASSENGERS WHO WERE EN ROUTE TO AIRPORTS THAT WERE SHUT DOWN DUE TO THE STORM. AIRPORT PERSONNEL SWUNG INTO ACTION, SUPPLYING STRANDED TRAVELERS WITH COTS, BLANKETS, PILLOWS, REFRESHMENTS, AND TRAVEL KITS.

"IT MADE A BAD SITUATION BEARABLE FOR OUR FAMILY," WROTE A GRATEFUL TRAVELER FROM NEW JERSEY. "IN FACT, WE REALLY HAD A GOOD TIME."

and dependable method of shipping goods and products across the United States and across the globe. By 1962, nearly half a million pounds of air freight moved through O'Hare, and before long a separate area for cargo had sprung up.

The airport's cargo operations began in the southwest corner of the field. United Airlines, then the leading domestic freight carrier, moved its cargo operation into a $3.5 billion building. TWA followed in 1965 with its own building that contained a fully mechanized cargo loading system. Other airlines and cargo haulers staked out locations.

By 1985, the airport had marked off a 240-acre plot of land in the southwest corner dedicated strictly to cargo operations, and soon a small collection of hangarlike buildings appeared, adding to the few already in place. The employees who worked in this sector of O'Hare dubbed it "Cargo City."

In 1988, American Airlines, officially the first tenant in Cargo City, opened a new $15 million facility. United Airlines constructed a $39 million facility. KLM Royal Dutch Airlines began operating out of its new building in May 1991. Air France and Lufthansa followed the next year. Today there are eight freight hangars, many the size of a giant warehouse.

Chicago soon surpassed New York in the volume of air cargo shipped, and by 1994 ranked third in the nation with 863,500 tons and fifth in the world with 521,100 tons of air freight.

Moving the Goods

Today Cargo City resembles a small industrial park, bustling with activity around the clock — although the busiest times occur from early morning until just after noon. Trucks of all sizes rumble in and out among waiting jumbo jets and air freighters, carrying everything from giant motors to tiny computers, made or assembled in the Midwest or arriving from a foreign country.

Air freight carriers such as Emery Air Freight, United Parcel Service (UPS), Federal Express, Airborne Express, Aer Lingus, China Air,

Iberia, Nippon Cargo, and Qantas are based at O'Hare, moving cargo to or from more than 140 domestic and 30 international destinations. Some companies are exclusively freight carriers, others have incorporated freighters in their fleets, and some, such as American Airlines, haul cargo on their passenger planes. "We stopped flying freighters in 1984," says American Airlines' Ed Martelle, manager of corporate communications for cargo. "Ninety percent of everything that moves can be loaded on the lower deck of a passenger plane."

About a third of the goods moving through O'Hare, much of it aboard passenger planes, is bound for major cities in the Midwest. "O'Hare is set up for it," says Tim Fleming of Strube Celery and Vegetables, a local wholesaler. During Chicago winters, cherries, apricots, red raspberries, specialty spices, and other perishable products arrive from warmer climates. The produce moves quickly to market. "There's never any real problem," Fleming adds. "The airport does a good job."

Airlines and air freight carriers maintain a discreet confidentiality about who their customers are and what they ship. Still, Cargo City regulars like to impress visitors with stories of the wide — and sometimes unusual — assortment of goods they see passing through every day. On any given morning, the holds of these planes might be loaded with fabrics, furniture, musical instruments, medical supplies, engines, or edibles. Visitors might catch a glimpse of cartons of fresh fish arriving from around the world destined for Chicago-area restaurants, thoroughbred horses on their way to Arlington Park Racetrack, chimpanzees heading for the Lincoln Park Zoo, or rare whales on the last leg of a journey to Chicago's Shedd Aquar-

ium. A few years ago, a herd of bison, signed for supporting roles in the Kevin Costner film *Dances with Wolves,* rode through O'Hare International, escorted not by cowboys and Indians but by Cargo City wranglers — sans horses.

In 1987, the U.S. Postal Service, still one of the largest freight customers of domestic air carriers, completed construction of a giant mail and parcel post station in Cargo City. This modern facility was expanded in 1993, and in 1994 processed more than 160,000 tons of mail, much of it carried by domestic airliners. But that is only part of the story.

Along with handling airmail, first class mail, priority mail, and parcel post shipments, one section of the building operates exactly like a neighborhood post office. Postal

BELOW: UNITED AIRLINES SUPPORTS ITS OWN $39 MILLION FACILITY IN O'HARE'S CARGO CITY. *PHOTO BY PETER J. SCHULZ, CITY OF CHICAGO, DEPT. OF AVIATION*

patrons drive in from Irving Park Road, enter the lobby, and buy stamps, mail letters or packages, or collect mail from post office boxes, utilizing the same services found in post offices in cities, towns, and villages across America.

O'Hare: A World-Class Airport

The airport and its landscape have undergone dramatic changes since President Kennedy's visit in 1963. A product of a revised blueprint, O'Hare International stands as a world-class airport in the heart of America, serving more than 67 million travelers per year — more than 184,000 per day — from both the United States and foreign countries. Twenty-eight commercial airlines and twenty cargo or freight airlines operate here.

O'Hare has grown through a succession of Chicago mayors: Kelly, Kennelly, Daley, Bilandic, Byrne, Washington, Sawyer, and its current mayor, Richard M. Daley. Each has contributed in some way to the improvement and development of O'Hare as a self-supporting, vital force in the economic health of the region.

O'Hare's emphasis on productivity, low operating costs, and customer service appears to be paying off. In a recent poll in *Business Traveler* magazine, O'Hare International was voted the best airport in North America. And *Fortune* magazine, citing the city's excellent transportation system, named Chicago the fifth-best city in the world in which to do business.

Chapter Four

Metropolis in the Heartland

When the title of "world's busiest airport" passed from Midway Airport to O'Hare International in 1962, part of Chicago's role at the time was perceived as a refueling stop, or a place to change planes and continue to other destinations. As aviation technology progressed, long-range jets eliminated the need for a refueling stop. However, O'Hare continued to roll up bigger numbers in flight operations and passenger volume. Part of the explanation lies in the city's central position on the map.

After World War II, with Chicago established as a transportation hub for railroads and airlines, the city established a reputation as a strong, vibrant urban center on the move in the heart of America, offering its resources, facilities, and potential to industry, commerce, trade — even to a fledgling world organization promoting peace and security.

In 1945, the United Nations was seeking a permanent headquarters site. A Chicago Citizens Committee embarked on a sales mission, trumpeting the city's accessibility from anywhere on the globe, and its North American location, "almost exactly at the centers of population

and industry . . . where the U.N. would have a greater opportunity than in any other location to influence strongly the public opinion of the United States."

Mayor Edward J. Kelly, traveling on American Airlines' first Chicago-to-London flight in 1945, personally courted the United Nations during the trip. In a letter to the U.N. Preparatory Commission, the mayor suggested that "beautiful Northerly Isle" would be an ideal site for the United Nations headquarters, "without cost, [and] permanently free of all taxes."

The offer apparently wasn't enough to tempt the United Nations. Eventually the U.N. chose New York as its site, and "beautiful Northerly Isle" later became Meigs Field, Chicago's lakefront airport. One can only speculate what might have been. Certainly the presence of the U.N. headquarters on Chicago's lakefront would have had a profound effect on the entire region.

LEFT: CHICAGO'S MAGNIFICENT SKYLINE AND RICH VARIETY OF ATTRACTIONS GREET THE MORE THAN 67 MILLION PASSENGERS WHO FLY IN AND OUT OF O'HARE AIRPORT EACH YEAR. *PHOTO BY PETER J. SCHULZ, CITY OF CHICAGO, DEPT. OF AVIATION*

Back in 1945, Chicago ignored the snub. There were other challenges to pursue, such as building Mayor Kelly's super airport. Today, over a half-century later, O'Hare International has continued without interruption as the world's busiest airport, serving both as a destination and as a gateway or connecting point to other cities. About 62 percent of the passengers arriving at O'Hare board connecting flights and never wander outside the airport grounds.

Master Plan

The foundation for O'Hare's success was laid by the city and the airlines in the early years by building a quality, world-class airport. These planners, working together, developed a master plan that would achieve major goals and improvements in stages. These included expanded roadways for better access to terminals, more parking space, a new air cargo complex, improved runways

and taxiways, a communications center, and, most important, a modern terminal complex.

From the onset, terminal designs that remotely resembled the old factory look of years ago were rejected. Planners sought architects with vision who created modern glass and steel structures that would last into the next century.

A major plank of the master plan also declared that city government and the air carriers would install a quality airport system that would not only oversee improvements but provide for the safety and convenience of passengers, from roadways to runways and into the skies. As a new century approaches, O'Hare has achieved recognition as a model for the aviation industry and has been acclaimed as a modern, world-class airport.

From modest beginnings in 1949, O'Hare has matured in size and stature while maintaining an uncongested and uncomplicated pattern of connected terminals. Travelers move with ease from one terminal to another, whereas in some large airports passengers must suffer the inconvenience of crowded bus rides, sometimes lasting more than half an hour, to reach a connecting flight in another terminal.

From its gleaming International Terminal 5 to its three ultramodern glass and steel domestic terminals, O'Hare, despite the volume of passenger traffic, usually seems uncrowded and uncluttered, even with the presence of the world's largest airline — United Airlines.

United We Stand

Identified as "Chicago's hometown airline," United is no stranger to the Windy City, the relationship extending back to the trailblazing days at Chicago Municipal Airport. United, created through a merger of four airline companies, and its dynamic president, William Patterson, worked closely with the city in the site selection and development of what later became O'Hare International Airport.

From its earliest days, United Airlines has played a leadership role in the development of commercial aviation as we know it today. United claims bragging rights to many "firsts": the world's first flight attendant service (1930); the first airline flight kitchen (1936); the first nonstop, coast-to-coast scheduled passenger flight (1955); the first to use satellite data communications in flight (1990); and the first U.S. airline to fly Boeing's 777, the most advanced passenger aircraft ever developed and the world's largest twin-engine jetliner (1995).

United Airlines, the world's largest air carrier (based on revenue passenger miles), employs nearly 16,000 people in the Chicago area. Worldwide, the employee-owned company has more than 550 aircraft

and 2,209 daily scheduled departures to 97 domestic and 39 international destinations. From its Chicago base at O'Hare, United (along with United Express) has grown to an average of 441 daily departures to 82 domestic and 10 international destinations.

The first terminal visitors see as they drive into O'Hare is United Airlines' $556.5 million Terminal 1, occupying some 85 acres in the space once held by the 1958-era International Terminal. United's new "Terminal for Tomorrow," dedicated on August 4, 1987, by the late Mayor Harold Washington, was drawn up as one of the central elements in the integrated master plan. Terminal 1 presented the flying public with a modern dimension in air travel with futuristic ticket pavilions, computer-

style ticketing, automated boarding passes, automated ticket dispensers, six curbside check-in stations, up-to-the-second flight information on monitors, and a laser-scanning baggage system that can process nearly 500 pieces of luggage a minute.

Terminal 1 comprises two 1,500-foot parallel concourses, each with barrel-vaulted glass ceilings. The contemporary glass and steel buildings, designed by Helmut Jahn, principal partner of Chicago's Murphy/Jahn architectural firm, are reminiscent of the railway stations of the past. One writer compared the terminal to the historic Galleria of Milan.

The two concourses, identified as B and C, have gates for 48 aircraft. Fourteen of the gates are located only 200 feet from curbside. The

parallel concourses have enough space between them to allow aircraft to taxi to or from gates in both directions. On average, 40,000 passengers move through this terminal each day.

Above the moving sidewalks that carry passengers from one concourse to another is a 744-foot-long, neon sculpture, *The Sky's the Limit*. During Terminal 1's grand opening, the sculpture quickly emerged as a star attraction in the new complex, featured nightly on local television newscasts.

Terminal 1's kinetic light sculpture displays a colorful program of continuously changing light patterns that shift through shades of indigo blue, green, red, yellow, and orange. California artist Michael Hayden, who designed the sculpture, says, "The combination of the changing light patterns on the ceiling, the backlit colors in the walls, and the synchronized music will result in an enjoyable and soothing experience for the passenger."

The American Way

Actually, the revamping of the original domestic terminals began in 1982 as part of the first stage in the O'Hare Development Program, the linchpin of the master plan. That same year, American Airlines, the nation's second-largest carrier, established O'Hare as its second-largest hub outside Dallas/Ft. Worth, the company's headquarters. Since its days at Chicago's Municipal Airport, American has been a partner in the growth and development of aviation in Chicago.

Today American Airlines carries more than 12 million passengers a

year and employs 11,000 people in its Chicago hub, operating 344 flights out of O'Hare daily. American Eagle, its sister airline, acts as a regional carrier and logs in an additional 150 flights every day. From O'Hare, American serves 74 cities nonstop.

American also boasts service to most major cities in Europe; in fact, it operates more flights out of O'Hare to Europe than New York's JFK airport. With 10 daily nonstops to Europe, along with service to Canada, Mexico, and the Caribbean, American's O'Hare base has opened a path to the world. American's status in worldwide service helped create the impetus for O'Hare's role as a key player in international air travel.

American modernized its entire O'Hare operation with new technology and developed a first-class terminal, capable of supporting the company's domestic and international market in Chicago. To upgrade and improve its operations in Terminal 3, American invested $500 million in the late 1980s.

Finally, the carrier's "Gateway to the World" terminal made its debut in 1990. Two spacious concourses, H and K, were crowned by ceilings of glass and steel. To accommodate its active flight schedule, American included space for 48 new gates, each roomy enough for gate personnel and passengers. American also introduced an underground baggage handling facility with seven miles of conveyors, controlled by 12 computers, that can handle 480 pieces of luggage per minute.

In 43 key airports around the world, American provides a special place for its business travelers, the Admiral's Club. In this "office away from the office," corporate representatives can relax, use telephones or electronic equipment, or meet with customers or associates to conduct business. With 33,000 square feet, the Admiral's Club at O'Hare bears the unique distinction of being the nation's largest VIP lounge.

About 16 airlines operate from O'Hare's domestic terminals. While they are smaller than United and American, they are no less significant in their service to the flying public. Among them, Delta Air Lines, the nation's third-largest air carrier, with its hub and headquarters in Atlanta, has filled a major role in serving southeast destinations from O'Hare. In Terminal 3, Delta operates from Concourse L, another major project that was launched in 1982 and completed in 1984.

Along with American, American Eagle, and Delta, four other airlines are based in Terminal 3: Air

Canada, TWA, Sun Country, and Qantas. Minneapolis-based Northwest Airlines, Continental, USAir, and America West operate, along with some United flights, from Terminal 2. Large or small, each airline has a voice in the operation of the airport.

While United's Terminal 1 basked in the pomp of its 1987 opening, city consultants embarked on the airport's most ambitious and long-awaited project: the giant new international facility that would replace the temporary International Terminal, occupying space in the ground floor of the parking building since 1985. (The original international terminal was torn down years earlier, and its space is now occupied by United Airlines.)

The design of a modern, technologically advanced international terminal was awarded to Perkins & Will Architects, assisted by Heard & Associates and by Consoer, Townsend and Associates. Several locations were considered before agreement was reached on a permanent site a half-mile east of the domestic complex. Ground was broken in July 1990 for this $618 million terminal, designated Terminal 5. It was built at no cost to taxpayers, having been financed through airport revenue bonds and federal grants.

A workforce of 15,000 participated in the new building's construction, more than a third of which

was composed of minorities — an accomplishment that won the construction team the Martin Luther King Economic Partnership Award.

Bringing the World to Chicago

In spring 1993, on the eve of the opening of the terminal, 1,800 guests attended a gala black-tie dinner ceremony. The Sister Cities program, linking Chicago with 12 cities around the world in education, art, and business, commissioned artists to visit the city and create murals for the arrivals corridor in the terminal. These 4-by-9-foot oil-on-canvas impressions of Chicago life remain on permanent display. "Chicago's sister cities," Mayor Richard M. Daley told guests, "remind us that this new terminal is not just about connecting flights, it's about connecting people."

Mayor Daley was joined by U.S. Transportation Secretary Federico Peña and airline officials for the opening of Terminal 5, a long, sweeping, arch-shaped building stretching end to end in a low-slung arc. Its interior of steel and concrete rose above terrazzo floors, while outside, a glimmering display of fluted metal panels and tinted glass greeted visitors.

During the ribbon-cutting ceremony, Secretary Peña declared that Terminal 5 represented a new benchmark in the aviation industry. "It's not only beautiful, it's convenient, efficient, and passenger-friendly," Peña said, "and it's going to bring the world to Chicago as never before."

An American Airlines flight from London and a United Airlines flight

ABOVE: THE 7,700-ACRE O'HARE AIRPORT SERVICES MAJOR DOMESTIC AND INTERNATIONAL CARRIERS. *PHOTO BY PETER J. SCHULZ, CITY OF CHICAGO, DEPT. OF AVIATION*

ALL ABOARD!

A KEY COMPONENT IN O'HARE'S $2 BILLION DEVELOPMENT PLAN WAS THE $127 MILLION AIRPORT TRANSPORT SYSTEM (ATS). THIS ELEVATED RAIL LINE WAS BUILT BY **MATRA** TRANSIT, INC., A UNITED STATES SUBSIDIARY OF **MATRA**, THE FRENCH-BASED FIRM THAT DEVELOPED SIMILAR SYSTEMS IN THAT COUNTRY. THE ATS, COMPLETED IN 1993, OPERATES 13 ELECTRONICALLY POWERED RAIL CARS ON 2.7 MILES OF ELEVATED TRACKS CONNECTING PASSENGERS, FREE OF CHARGE, WITH FOUR TERMINALS AND THE LONG-TERM PARKING FACILITY. IN ADDITION TO MOVING PEOPLE, THE RAIL LINE LESSENS CONGESTION AND AIR POLLUTION.

With Terminal 5's laser-reading baggage sorting system, luggage usually arrives even before passengers reach the carousels. Passengers retrieve their luggage from one of nine luggage carousels, more than double the number in the old terminal. Once they have claimed luggage, passengers continue through Customs and proceed to a spacious "meeter-greeter" lobby. For those continuing to domestic locations, 24 counters are available for rechecking baggage.

from Paris taxied in together as the first arrivals at Terminal 5. Secretary Peña and Mayor Daley welcomed passengers as they deplaned and presented commemorative passports marking the opening of the terminal.

Outside, the terminal occupies approximately 100 acres. Inside, it measures about 1.2 million square feet, roughly three times the size of its predecessor and stretching more than a city block. Like the domestic complex, the terminal employs a two-level-approach road system. A four-lane roadway leads to the upper level for departures, while a six-lane roadway on the lower level services arrivals.

As for the inspection service stops that international airports require — Immigration and Naturalization, Customs, Department of Agriculture, Fish and Wildlife, and Public Health — what was once a long and sometimes exhausting chore has been converted into a quick and efficient process. Deplaning passengers proceed to the lower level, where 68 booths are capable of processing 4,000 passengers an hour.

ABOVE: DELTA AIR LINES, OPERATING OUT OF O'HARE'S TERMINAL 3, IS THE COUNTRY'S THIRD-LARGEST AIRLINE. *PHOTO BY BRUCE LEIGHTY©/IMAGE FINDERS.* BELOW: U.S. TRANSPORTATION SECRETARY FEDERICO PEÑA (LEFT) AND MAYOR RICHARD DALEY (RIGHT) CUT THE RIBBON AT THE OPENING CEREMONY FOR THE INTERNATIONAL TERMINAL. *PHOTO BY PETER J. SCHULZ, CITY OF CHICAGO, DEPT. OF AVIATION*

Arriving in a strange country or a city can sometimes be overwhelming for a traveler, but O'Hare has made arrivals friendlier and less traumatic by implementing a changing signage program on the lower level of the terminal. Passengers are greeted by signs in 17 languages, displaying a cordial welcome and important directions. And to ease a traveler's load during the short trip through the terminal, carts are available to carry personal belongings and luggage.

Other amenities located in Terminal 5 include VIP lounges, two banks for foreign currency exchange, a duty-free shop, restaurants, additional shops, rest rooms, and concessions bearing a distinct Chicago flavor such as Pizzeria Uno, Gold Coast Dogs, Lou Mitchell's Express, and McDonald's.

In a tribute to its interior architecture, Terminal 5 captured three prestigious awards from the American Institute of Architects' "Design Excellence" series in 1994.

In early 1996, 29 foreign airlines operated from Terminal 5. British Airways, which one writer called the "king" of international air routes, has at least one nonstop flight to London daily from O'Hare during the off season, and two a day during the peak summer travel season.

Taking the "El" Train

Before construction on Terminal 5 began, the city, airlines, and airport consultants decided on the installation of an elevated transit system, a rail line known as an Airport Transit System, or ATS. The ATS would carry passengers free of charge between international and domestic terminals and parking lots. Along with its basic task of moving people, the rail line would minimize the number of cars, buses, and taxis entering the core roadways, lessening congestion and air pollution.

O'Hare's $127 million ATS was built by MATRA Transit, Inc., a U.S. subsidiary of MATRA, the French-based firm that has developed similar systems in Lille, Strasbourg, Bordeaux, and Toulouse, France. In the United States, MATRA has established a rail transit system in Jacksonville, Florida.

Construction on the ATS, a key component in O'Hare's $2 billion development plan, was completed in 1993. ATS trains run on 2.7 miles of elevated track and stop at five stations connecting passengers with terminals 1, 2, 3, International Terminal 5, and the long-term parking facility. About 57 passengers and their luggage can fit nicely in each of the 13 electronically powered vehicles. All trains and stations are accessible to persons with disabilities.

Boarding rail cars, passengers may find the ATS a little unconventional in that there is no engineer or conductor aboard. The trains are fully automated, operated from a remote control room. Trains move from station to station at a speed of 35 mph. Travel time between domestic terminals takes about two to three minutes each, and from the domestic core to the International Terminal, about five minutes.

Another innovation in 1992 has improved airport security and communications. In this safety-conscious industry, when the times demand vigilance, an airport can offer an added level of security by monitoring and responding quickly to any threatening incident.

The federal government and air carriers installed a $40 million Communications Center at O'Hare.

The center monitors airport activity around the clock through a network of 500 television cameras, each placed in a strategic location or critical point of entry. With any situation that arises — an automobile accident on an access road, a medical emergency, a fire in a terminal, or an unauthorized person attempting to enter a secured area — response will be fast and decisive.

Once emergency crews have been dispatched, additional support is available from the center. Essential information on potential dangers can be called up on a computer and relayed to personnel in the field. In a fire, for example, firefighters can thwart additional trouble when they know the location of fuel tanks or utility lines. And, finally, the Communications Center, with input from experts in all fields, can coordinate a plan of action for any situation.

The center is also a clearinghouse for incidents that are phoned in. If someone at the airport dials the 911 emergency number, the call goes through directly to the O'Hare Communications Center instead of a

building downtown, saving precious time. Personnel in the center can dispatch police or fire units based right on the airport grounds.

O'Hare's Communications Center, replacing an earlier system that was spread over four locations, has consolidated all critical communications in one place. The center stands as a model for the nation, and several airports have either installed or are planning similar communications centers.

O'Hare International's state-of-the-art terminals, unique passenger facilities and services, ATS rail system, advanced Communications Center, and resident airlines explain in part why the airport is the busiest in the world. The other half of the story is found in the city of Chicago and its suburbs, and what they offer in facilities, accommodations, tourism, and leisure activities.

Conventional Wisdom

From its airport to its convention halls, hotels, baseball parks, and museums, Chicago seems to have something for everyone, for those who live here and especially for

those who are just "stopping by." The 67.2 million travelers using the airport each year have helped confirm O'Hare as the world's busiest airport, and Chicago as one of the most attractive destinations for business and pleasure. About 55 percent of the passengers arriving at O'Hare are business travelers, and Chicago has proven that it has the experience and the know-how to serve their needs.

Five minutes from O'Hare Airport, the Rosemont Convention Center, boasting six halls, a conference center, and 600,000 square feet of space for trade shows, expositions, and conventions, schedules 80 to 100 events annually, drawing visitors and exhibitors from Chicago, the Midwest, and around the world. Trade groups at Rosemont in 1996 literally covered the spectrum and included International Craft Exposition, Petroleum Marketers, Housewares, Labelexpo, Quality Expo Time, Electrical Manufacturing and Coil Winding, and Chicago Midwest Bicycle. Among the consumer shows open to the public were the Antique Show, Trucks America,

Franchise Expo, Model and Hobby, Boat Show, and Skokie Valley Kennel Club.

The Chicago Sport Fishing, Travel, and Outdoors Show at Rosemont attracts about 65,000 people each year. And every February, Steve Sidari's Chicago Golf Show provides national manufacturers, retailers, specialty shops, and resort representatives a chance to display their wares to more than 35,000 golf enthusiasts who come to the Rosemont Center in the dead of winter searching for the holy grail of golf. They can browse, buy golf equipment, plan a dream vacation, or partake in golf clinics at the 300 corporate booths.

McCormick Place, the mammoth lakefront convention center a few minutes south of downtown Chicago, has entertained major conventions, shows, and exhibits for more than three decades. Today it is the largest exhibition and meeting facility in North America, with 1.5 million square feet of exposition space, 52 meeting rooms, four theaters, and five banquet rooms.

Each winter, the Chicago Automobile Show transforms McCormick Place into a glamorous auto showroom for the public. Industry moguls unveil their newest model cars and sample public opinion on futuristic cars that may or may not see an assembly line. While salesmen exalt the virtues of the cars, prospective buyers climb into the vehicles for a hands-on test of new features. Nearly one million people filed through McCormick Place in February 1996 for a sneak preview of the industry's latest designs and styles.

LEFT: BRITISH AIRWAYS IS ONE OF 29 FOREIGN CARRIERS OPERATING OUT OF O'HARE INTERNATIONAL. *PHOTO BY INDEX STOCK.* BELOW: BOAT TOURS ON THE CHICAGO RIVER, OFFERED MAY TO OCTOBER, PROVIDE VISITORS WITH MAGNIFICENT VIEWS OF THE WORLD-RENOWNED CHICAGO SKYLINE. *PHOTO BY BRAD CROOKS*©

Other regulars at the giant exhibition hall include the Chicago Boat, Sport, and RV Show, the Housewares Show, and a diverse assortment of trade and industry shows. In 1995, the American Booksellers Association chose McCormick Place for its annual convention. More than 40,000 publishers, authors, agents, collectors, and book lovers gathered over three days at the lakefront hall. The ABA apparently liked the facili-

ties so much they closed the book on rotating their convention sites, and, for the next decade, at least, the ABA will settle into McCormick Place for its annual gathering.

Navy Pier, a Chicago landmark jutting out into Lake Michigan on the Near North Side, has joined the competition for convention business. The pier has been completely refurbished and proudly claims it can handle any event from a black-tie affair to a flower show. In February 1996, while the weather outside was frightful, Navy Pier held an old-fashioned County Fair, featuring rides, carnival attractions, arts and crafts, live entertainment, and traditional county fair exhibits. Three weeks later, the National Fly-Fishing trade show was in full swing, displaying the newest rods and other fishing equipment, and conducting workshops for anglers.

Come summer, visitors can climb aboard and ride Navy Pier's "Giant Wheel," the world's largest Ferris wheel, standing 15 stories high. (In case you didn't know, the Ferris wheel was first introduced in Chicago more than half a century ago.)

For an unusual bit of excitement and interest, visitors can observe the spirited action on the trading floors of Chicago's key financial institutions, the Chicago Stock Exchange, the Board of Trade, or the Mercantile Exchange, all in downtown Chicago.

A Taste of Chicago

For dining, Chicago loves to show off its restaurants and cafes, where diners can savor the finest steaks or

sample the city's ethnic flavor in some of the most interesting restaurants found anywhere in the world. Chicago's list of eating establishments reads like a United Nations roster, with all varieties of Asian, American, French, German, Italian, Indian, and Spanish foods, created by chefs who work in kitchens around the Loop, the Gold Coast, Milwaukee Avenue, Greek Town, Little Village, Chinatown, and beyond. And closer to the airport, more than 50 restaurants, offering both fine and casual dining, appeal to visitors and locals alike.

An array of shopping centers and plazas also attracts visitors, beginning with the city's well-known State Street in the Loop, and continuing with North Michigan Avenue's Magnificent Mile, Ford City, and the suburban shops in Northbrook Court, Oak Brook, Old Orchard, Edens Plaza, and Woodfield Mall. Those who merely want to window shop can try the showroom floors of the Merchandise Mart or take a tour

of the Apparel Center, both in the downtown area.

Cultural Cachet

Chicago is rich in cultural attractions. One of its most cherished is the Chicago Symphony Orchestra, now in its second century of live performances for Chicago audiences. Since its inception in 1891, the CSO has steadily advanced to become one of the world's great orchestras, under the direction of the music world's greatest conductors.

Younger Chicagoans may not remember the orchestra's Fritz Reiner, whose recordings in the 1950s are still considered performance hallmarks, but the names

of Sir George Solti and Daniel Barenboim are certainly household words. Maestro Solti joined the orchestra in 1969 and two years later launched the first CSO international tour. With it came international fame and recognition for the deserving orchestra.

In 1991, after 22 years, Sir George moved to the post of Music Director Laureate, and a new collaboration was launched with Daniel Barenboim, the CSO's ninth director. Under Maestro Barenboim's direction, the orchestra has logged four highly acclaimed international tours. Today, 105 years after its founding, the CSO continues to be recognized the world over as one of the finest musical ensembles ever to perform.

Another Chicago treasure, the Lyric Opera, performs an annual production of a select group of operas, featuring visiting artists who perform with a resident cast. In March 1996, the Lyric Opera accomplished the seemingly impossible task of staging Richard Wagner's grand production, *The Ring of the Nibelung*. Opera devotees know the production simply as "The Ring": four operas performed over six days and lasting a total of nearly 16 hours. Most of the 42,000 seats for this $6.5 million production were sold seven months in advance.

Chicago loves its music, in all varieties, from barbershop harmony to rock to bluegrass. Jazz — which music historian Dave Dexter, Jr., called "America's only true original art form" — still flourishes in the Windy City. Chicago holds a revered place in the history and evolution of jazz, and, while many jazz landmarks are gone, Chicago carries on the tradition in nightspots such as Andy's and Fitzgerald's, and in lounges of some major hotels. And every summer, the Chicagoland Jazz Festival entertains fans at free concerts in Grant Park.

Another summer pastime guaranteed to please can be found north of the city at Ravinia Park, a 46-minute train ride from downtown Chicago. Here families, music lovers, and lovers in general gather for picnics — many bring wine, fine foods, and candelabras — while savoring the music of top artists in concerts under the stars.

Art of the Matter

Chicago's museums offer a continuing parade of cultural and educational programs and exhibits. In 1995, the Art Institute of Chicago, a Michigan Avenue landmark downtown, presented the largest exhibition of French artist Claude Monet's work ever assembled. Nearly 965,000 visitors attended, and more than two-thirds came from outside the metropolitan area, representing every state and 16 foreign countries. Four out of five visitors stated the Monet exhibit influenced their decision to come to Chicago. Eleven Chicago hotels offered special packages to guests attending the exhibit during its July–November run.

The Monet exhibit proved to be the most successful ticketed exhibition in the Art Institute's 113-year history. The exhibit's total direct impact on the city was estimated at approximately $140 million, spent on hotels, shopping, restaurants, and transportation. The total economic impact, estimated by the Regional Economics Applications Laboratory — and taking in the ripple effect in other business activity, entertainment, and city and state tax revenues — reached $393 million.

In late 1996, lines were forming at the Art Institute for another special exhibit, featuring the works of Edgar Degas. Institute officials predicted that a half million would view the collection of this French impressionist by the time the show concluded in January 1997.

As residents can attest, the Field Museum of Natural History, the Museum of Science and Industry, the Chicago Historical Society, the

Oriental Institute Museum, the Adler Planetarium, the Shedd Aquarium, and the Harold Washington Library are "musts" on any traveler's agenda. Many tourists enjoy side trips to the Lincoln Park Zoo, the Brookfield Zoo, and the Morton Arboretum. The Shubert Theater, the Chicago Theater, and the Auditorium Theater offer stage productions year round. In recent years, such traveling shows as *Les Miserables* and *Miss Saigon* played long engagements in the Auditorium Theater. The Goodman Theater (adjacent to the Art Institute) has seen many of its drama students advance to the professional ranks in the theater and in motion pictures. Second City has achieved fame as a springboard for stars such as the late John Belushi, Bill Murray, Shelly Long, and George Wendt.

Hollywood, noting Chicago's landmarks and neighborhoods, has also chosen Chicago and employed local talent for many productions filmed in the city, including such

ABOVE: THE CHICAGO SYMPHONY ORCHESTRA. *PHOTO BY JIM STEERE*©

recent hits as *Home Alone, While You Were Sleeping,* and *The Fugitive.*

On an educational level, Chicago lists several major institutions of higher learning: the University of Chicago, DePaul University, Loyola University, Northwestern, Roosevelt University, and the University of Illinois at Chicago. The city also claims several university-affiliated hospitals and medical centers.

Architectural Gems

Chicago contains a wealth of architectural gems. William Le Baron Jenney built the world's first skyscraper in Chicago in 1884, launching the "Chicago School" of architecture, which broke with tradition. Throughout the city are the architectural legacies of Louis Sullivan, Dankmar Adler, Daniel Burnham, Frank Lloyd Wright, Helmut Jahn,

Stanley Tigerman, Ludwig Mies van der Rohe, Bruce Graham, Walter Netsch, Adrianne Smith, Lawrence Perkins, and Philip Will.

Today, the central city flaunts a panorama of classic old and new skyscrapers, dominated by the Sears Tower, the world's second-tallest building (a pair of Malaysian towers snatched the title away in the spring of 1996), the Hancock Building, and the Amoco Building.

For many visitors, the first impression of Chicago may come with the view of its magnificent skyline and lush perimeter of lakefront parks from the air. While other cities have squandered their waterfronts on industry and factories, Chicagoans fiercely guard their lakefront as though it were the soul of the city, a green expanse of playgrounds, band shells, stadiums, and museums against a backdrop of majestic skyscrapers.

On Soldier Field, the Romanesque outdoor stadium on the lakefront, the 1985 Super Bowl champion Chicago Bears battle NFL opponents each fall. In 1994, Soldier Field also played host to the World Cup Soccer Games. O'Hare International rolled out the red carpet for teams and fans arriving for the games. Airport employees enrolled in training classes, conducted by Walt Disney University and the World Cup Host Committee, to assist visitors. The airport terminals were draped with huge team banners and flags of World Cup competitors, and students of the mayor's Gallery 37 High School Arts Employment Program painted benches in each participating country's colors. Airport staff assigned to information booths distributed more than 100,000 pieces of material printed in several languages. An International Music Festival, sponsored by Coca-Cola, welcomed arriving passengers in Terminal 5.

World Cup Soccer doesn't come every year, but there are plenty of other sports on the menu. The NBA champion Chicago Bulls, led by superstar Michael Jordan, thrill basketball fans at the United Center, the palace that replaced historic Chicago Stadium. During the NHL hockey season, the center is converted into an ice rink for Chicago Blackhawks home games. In summer 1996, the United Center was transformed into a political arena when it opened its doors to thousands of delegates to the Democratic National Convention.

Chicago is one of the few cities that supports two major league baseball teams. The White Sox play at the new Comiskey Park, built at the same southside location as the old park, and the Cubs play at venerable Wrigley Field, which has maintained its old-fashioned charm despite the addition of lights.

The metropolitan area claims more golf courses than any city in the world. Open to the public, Cog Hill's famed Dubsdread Golf Course in Lemont, southwest of the city, is the tournament site of the Motorola Western Open every summer. Medina Country Club, in the western suburb of Medina, has played host to many historic U.S. Opens and Seniors tournaments.

Racing fans are treated to a year-round program of horse racing at four suburban tracks. In late summer, Arlington International Race Course attracts champion Thoroughbred horses, breeders, and racing fans from around the world for the "Arlington Million" classic. Other popular tracks such as Hawthorne Park Race Course, Sportsman's Park, and Maywood Park offer Thoroughbred and harness racing.

From its airport to its convention halls, stadiums to museums, Chicago's wide range of amenities is among the numerous reasons air carriers have designated O'Hare International as a primary connecting point and a destination of choice — the quality of the airport and its geographical location are also key factors. The airlines have been partners with the city in improving the airport and supporting facilities. As a result, O'Hare is the engine that drives the economy of the region — one can only speculate where the city would be without this giant in its midst.

Chapter Five

A Vision for the Future

In February 1996, President Jacques Chirac of France flew from Washington, D.C., to Chicago to conduct an informal trade mission promoting the products of France to Chicago's business and political community. During a dinner at the Art Institute of Chicago, President Chirac complimented Chicago as "a city whose nobility and grandeur are the symbol of America which has made us dream and which still makes us dream."

A significant part of Chicago's continuing greatness can be attributed to O'Hare International. In just four decades, the presence of O'Hare has inspired a dynamic transformation of the entire region. Expressways and interstate highways leading to the heart of Chicago, its suburbs, and destinations in surrounding states circulate around the airport. In every direction, once-empty fields have blossomed into a montage of aesthetically pleasing corporate office buildings, plush hotels, convention centers, and commercial and industrial sites.

Given the challenge of building a new airport following World War II, the city of Chicago, along with the air carriers, created the essen-

tial element that has sparked the region's economy. Chicago is the home of such corporate giants as Motorola, Amoco, Ameritech, WMX Technologies, Sears, Abbott Laboratories, McDonald's, Illinois Tool Works, Sara Lee, Baxter International, Walgreen, Allstate, Unicom, R.R. Donnelley & Sons, Quaker Oats, Wm. Wrigley, CNA Financial Corp., Morton International, General Instrument Corp., and hundreds of other companies, large and small. Many corporations, such as auto giants Ford and Chrysler, have plants or branch offices nearby. More than 500 foreign-owned businesses now call the Chicago area home, chiefly because of O'Hare's strategic position on the global map.

Together, this multitude of corporate entities, combined with local companies that service Chicago's airports and air carriers, have produced jobs. A 1993 study by Massachusetts-based National

LEFT: STRATEGIC LONG-RANGE PLANNING, SOLID RESOURCES, AND A COMMITMENT TO SERVICE ENSURE O'HARE'S PLACE AS ONE OF THE WORLD'S PREMIER AIRPORTS THROUGHOUT THE NEXT CENTURY. *PHOTO COURTESY OF LANDRUM & BROWN*

ABOVE: THIS SHOP IS JUST ONE OF MANY QUALITY SHOPPING DESTINATIONS FOUND THROUGHOUT O'HARE. *PHOTO BY BRUCE LEIGHTY©/IMAGE FINDERS*

Economic Research Associates indicated that Chicago's airports created more than 340,000 jobs, most of them evenly split between the city and suburbs. O'Hare International itself employs more than 50,000 people.

People associated with aviation make up a significant part of the economic chain that extends through communities near the airport: airline executives, pilots, flight attendants, air controllers, operations employees, meteorologists, mechanics, in-flight meal suppliers, fuel providers, cargo handlers, electricians, plumbers, skilled tradesmen, firemen, policemen, medical personnel, communications workers, custodial workers, truckers, dispatchers, parking attendants, taxi and limousine drivers, concessionaires, skycaps, construction workers, architects, and more.

Each year, billions of dollars in wages, benefits, and other personal income from airport-connected jobs filter through every communi-

ty in the Chicago metro area. The city's Department of Aviation calculates the regional economic impact figure of its airports at $14.7 billion annually.

As a drawing card for both domestic and foreign business interests, O'Hare International has played a key role in the dramatic rise in population in nearby cities, towns, and villages. Consider that in 1950 — the year following O'Hare's first dedication ceremony — the combined population of the surrounding communities of Arlington Heights, Bensenville, Des Plaines, Elk Grove Village, Franklin Park, Niles, Park Ridge, Rosemont, Schiller Park, and Wood Dale numbered fewer than 60,000 people. In the 1990 U.S. census, these same suburbs, entwined with the airport either through business, employment, or housing, expanded by 385 percent to a population of 290,725!

This airport would seem to be a desirable asset to the economic livelihood of any region. Yet O'Hare's presence after more than

40 years in this once-rural area has never been fully accepted or welcomed — despite the fact that the airport generates an estimated $100,000 of income for every nine arrivals and departures.

Sounds of Silence

The most frequent objection to the airport is aircraft noise and its affect on schools and homes. For more than 13 years, the city of Chicago, as manager and developer with the airlines of this giant airport, has been targeted in the courts and on the political front by suburban groups.

While the aviation industry searched for technical solutions, some relief from jetliner noise was found in soundproofing school buildings and homes along flight paths. To this end, Chicago has initiated the nation's largest sound-proofing program for schools, homes, and other buildings near O'Hare Airport and Midway Airport as well. This policy, which continues today, was discredited as insufficient by the same airport opponents in the northwest suburbs.

Finally, a ray of hope in the dispute appeared in February 1996. After years of confrontation, officials announced that all parties in a 1989 school soundproofing lawsuit had reached an official agreement, one that would provide additional soundproofing for schools in six districts in nearby DuPage County. And the city even included some private schools in DuPage County.

Lee Daniels, Republican Speaker of the Illinois House of Representatives, said he hoped the 1996 agreement represented "a new era of cooperation between the city-owned airport and suburban communities." As for the constant feuding, Daniels declared that "confrontation . . . is not the best way to solve the aggravating noise problems."

Chicago Mayor Richard M. Daley said the agreement "demonstrates the city's absolute, continued commitment to addressing noise at area schools." The city says that as of 1996, it has offered $236 million "over the next 10 years for sound-proofing and other eligible noise reduction programs." Chicago also embarked on a large-scale plan with the federal government to soundproof more than 4,500 suburban homes near the airport at a cost of $90 million.

The renovations have been well received. "It feels like a blanket

over the whole house," said Renee Miakowski of Schiller Park, whose home was one of five initially tested for sound insulation. "It's such a difference. Now they're landing over our home, and I don't even notice."

Another resolution focuses on a noise monitoring system. In 1995, Chicago introduced an independently operated, permanent sound monitoring system to track aircraft operations and flight patterns. Monitors at 36 key locations near O'Hare and 12 near Midway will measure and track excessive aircraft noise, and identify the communities affected. Collected data will help the FAA and the airlines route planes over less-populated areas. Whenever possible, planes are already steered to flight patterns over industrial corridors and forest preserves. Older, noisier jets are banned from night flights. The first phase of the monitoring system was completed in late 1995.

Much of the airport's battle against noise had been guided by Aviation Commissioner David Mosena. In late summer 1996, Mayor Daley tapped Mosena to take charge of the Chicago Transit Authority, and appointed Mary Rose Loney, Director of Philadelphia's International Airport, to replace Mosena. Loney, who served

as first deputy commissioner at O'Hare during the late 1980s, is a veteran airport professional whose other posts included San Jose, Las Vegas, Albuquerque, and Dallas–Ft. Worth. Loney has pledged to stimulate the O'Hare Noise Commission program, which some suburban interests have boycotted.

"Through the issuance of $250 billion in bonds . . . we now have the financial resources and the commitment to launch this program expeditiously," Commissioner Loney explains. "I hope this will be an incentive for our surrounding neighbors to sit down with us and become a part of this."

The cost for antinoise measures is presently financed chiefly by bonds, federal funds, and a passenger facility charge at airports throughout the Chicago area. The ultimate resolution, however, remains with the aircraft designers and those who manufacture jet engines.

New FAA legislation requires that airlines convert their fleets to the quieter Stage 3 jets with noise suppressors and antipollution systems by 1999. As airlines purchase this new equipment, the noise problem is abating. The city's Department of Aviation, citing the arrival of these new and quieter jets, has projected an 80 percent decline in the number of homes affected by noise.

RIGHT: A NETWORK OF EXPRESSWAYS LINKS O'HARE TO CITIES THROUGHOUT THE MIDWEST. *PHOTO BY WILLIAM A. HOLMES©/IMAGE FINDERS*

Gateway to the World

O'Hare today is not only a gateway to the Midwest and the nation but also to the entire world. O'Hare now ranks as the second-largest gateway over the Atlantic, after New York's JFK, with nonstop service to major cities in England, Ireland, Scotland, Italy, France, Belgium, Holland, Germany, Switzerland, Denmark, Sweden, Poland, the Czech Republic, and Russia. The airport's future, according to one airport executive, rests in exploring a vast, untapped international market.

The capability to reach foreign markets with direct flights can have a profound effect in building a local economy. Consider what happened in Atlanta: Before that city had direct service to London, Atlanta claimed 50 British-based companies or companies doing business in Great Britain. Four years later, with long-range jets and direct flights to London, the Atlanta area claimed 250 companies with British connections.

The impressive roster of Chicago-based firms with foreign connections broadened its influence and presence in overseas markets in manufacturing and sales, knowing that a first-class international airport was there to support it. Other corporations are following suit. "Corporations are becoming more global," says Barrett Murphy, director of marketing for the city's Department of Aviation, citing one Chicago company that put up 30 plants a year in foreign countries. "A vice president must visit each plant once a month. Their chairman visits once a year — the chairman is their most valuable commodity. This company needs direct service to the closest point possible to get their executives in and out quickly." Noting that O'Hare has two flights a day to Tokyo, Murphy adds, "We could probably handle four every day, and they are extremely profitable. On every Tokyo flight, United Airlines sells about 200 business-class seats."

In aviation circles, it is estimated that 47 percent of the United States populace has flown at least once in their lives. In Japan, it's about 27 percent, and in China, about .001. Chinese tourists and entrepreneurs, with no freeways, interstates, or national highway system, may well look to the skies when defining their transportation futures. The thought of that potential market — and others — excites the imaginations of airline executives. O'Hare is pursuing more distant, smaller markets. Beyond Tokyo are China, Malaysia, the Philippines, Thailand, and others. With its global position secure and a strong corporate population in residence, O'Hare fits snugly into the foreign market equation.

As the United States continues to sign bilateral agreements with other nations, O'Hare will have a definite advantage, especially in flying to Asia. Planes leaving O'Hare fly over polar routes. Many destinations are closer, and the trip faster and more efficient, for flights leaving from Chicago than those departing from Los Angeles for the same destinations. Best of all, a 747-400 jet with daily service from Asia or Europe brings in $400 to $600 million to the Chicago area economy.

And from Boeing Aircraft comes exciting news of two new planes soon to be joining the world's airlines: the 9,200-mile-range 747-500 and the 560-seat 747-600. "We want to attract international carriers," says Murphy, "so they recognize that O'Hare is the premier airport with the best connections to anyplace. And we have a new International Terminal."

Making Concessions

With this vast market on the horizon — and 184,000 passengers moving through the airport each day — O'Hare has been improving its facilities to maintain the leadership position it earned in service to air travelers. For example, the city is boosting its concession facilities by 76 percent, adding more shops and restaurants — many with a distinct Chicago flavor — to serve visitors with time to spare as they await their flights.

Passengers can spend from one to two hours checking luggage, traveling to gates, waiting for planes, or transferring to other airlines. To better accommodate these passengers — and about 13,000 other "meet-and-greet" people every day — Chicago has promised to bring a broad range of quality shops and dining facilities to O'Hare International.

McDonald's, the food chain serving 33 million people a day in 18,000 restaurants in 90 countries, has been operating restaurants in airports around the world for more than 15 years. With corporate offices in nearby Oak Brook, Illinois, McDonald's opened three restaurants in O'Hare's domestic terminals in summer 1996, with two to follow. Joining McDonald's will be Connie's Pizza, a popular Chicago establishment. Air Venture, W H Smith, and Grabur International have established Waterstone's Booksellers, a premier bookstore, at O'Hare in four locations, along with two new CD emporiums, The Wall music stores. W H Smith, operating at O'Hare for 10 years, will open six additional news and gift stores in the domestic terminals.

Starbucks, the popular Seattle-based chain of coffee bars, boasts nine locations in O'Hare. A new Goose Island Bar, a spin-off of Chicago's Goose Island Brewery, is serving thirsty customers in Terminal 3. Other newcomers include Fresh Departure snack bars and Quick Connection food and beverage stands. One of the oldest vendors at the airport, the O'Hare Heel Bar and Valet Shop, a minority-owned shoe shine and valet service, will upgrade its existing shops.

Passengers will soon be able to relax in new food courts, beverage stands, and shopping areas, accessible from domestic terminals. Some existing establishments will be expanded, and the city will build out from some terminals, adding new space for vendors — without destroying the character of the terminal complex.

O'Hare has pledged to bring shopping opportunities to its visitors with better merchandise and national brands at competitive prices. All of O'Hare's food and shopping concessionaires have agreed to implement a policy of street pricing, that is, charging

customers the same price or lower than what they would normally pay in the city.

Other improvements are already in evidence around the airport, and some are on the drawing board. A sleek new FAA control tower, which began operating in 1996, can be seen on the approaches to the airport, rising in a slender, flowerlike silhouette 260 feet above the terminals. Its facade, composed of blue-green glass, blends with the sky as it flares to an expansive "cab" where FAA controllers direct aircraft.

In the northeast corner of O'Hare, 356 acres of land occupied by Air Force reserve units will soon be available for development. In 1995, the U.S. Base Closure and Realignment Commission voted to disband the Air Force's 928th Airlift Wing and relocate the 126th Airlift Wing of the Air National Guard to a new location. The long-delayed transfer of the property where the Douglas Aircraft plant once stood will open prime land for industry, generating more jobs and more dollars for the local economy.

Playing Politics

"In Chicago, there's nothing like a good political fight," goes the saying. The recent controversy over Chicago's airports added to the city's rich political lore. In 1996, Mayor Daley unveiled plans to convert Meigs Field, the 91-acre lakefront airport on Northerly Island, to a nature park with sandy beaches, wetlands, a museum, and gardens, part of the city's new "museum campus." Protests rolled in

OPPOSITE AND BELOW: O'HARE INTERNA-TIONAL AIRPORT OFFERS DAILY NONSTOP SERVICE TO MANY EUROPEAN DESTINA-TIONS INCLUDING FRANCE AND HOLLAND. *PHOTOS BY MICHAEL PHILIP MANHEIM©/ IMAGE FINDERS (OPPOSITE) AND INDEX STOCK© (BELOW)*

from private pilots and commercial fliers. Republican Governor Jim Edgar, feuding with the mayor over a new football stadium for the Chicago Bears and a third major airport, joined the fray. The battle was played out in several courts, but the city prevailed, and Meigs was closed on September 30, with bulldozers standing by to raze airport buildings. However, an appellate court ruling temporarily banned the city from demolishing or removing any structures, pending hearings of all appeals. The airport's fate rests in one of three places: the courts, the legislature, or the negotiating table.

Before the Meigs controversy erupted, Midway Airport found itself thrown into the ongoing political war between the mayor and the governor. The revered southwestside airport would once again be tested, this time in a battle involving an airport that doesn't exist.

The early 1960s, when major airlines deserted Midway for O'Hare's longer, jet-accommodating runways, were tough years for Midway, but the airport somehow survived. While O'Hare was booming, Midway followed the peaks and valleys of air travel. By 1991 it seemed to be riding high,

thanks to the success of Midway Airlines, a new carrier. Then, without warning, the airport suffered a major blow — Midway Airlines abruptly ceased operations. The airport management watched helplessly as both jobs and airplanes disappeared.

Once referred to as "the busiest square mile in the country," Midway was serving only four carriers in 1992, but, thanks to a new surge in start-up carriers and lower air fares, managed still another comeback. This 70-year-old airport, with as many lives as a cat, proved an ideal launch pad for new airlines. By 1996, 19 carriers were flying in and out of the airport, offering 250 flights a day to 70 cities. Midway's resurgence created 50,000 jobs for the city and surrounding suburbs.

In light of the airport's new prosperity, city officials decided the aging terminal would have to be replaced. Not even a few facelifts along the way had sustained the 50-year-old terminal. City officials and executives from three of Midway's leading carriers — Southwest, Continental, and American Trans Air — announced plans for a new terminal with bigger gates and hold areas. The project, involving substantial investment, demonstrated the airlines' confidence that Midway would remain an integral part of Chicago's airport system into the next century.

advanced this proposal despite a clear forewarning from the airlines that they didn't want a Peotone airport and wouldn't move there if it were built. Mayor Daley, with O'Hare's future in mind, also opposed the governor's airport.

Then came the shock: Midway Airport's largest carrier, Southwest Airlines, already with a significant financial stake in the airport, stated flatly that it would be forced to leave Chicago if an airport were built in Peotone. This announcement sparked questions about Midway's new terminal and the airport's future. However, in the fall of 1996, the city moved forward with its plan for the new terminal, erasing any doubts about Midway's status in Chicago's aviation future.

The most recent installment of the ongoing political battles over Chicago's airports centered around O'Hare International Airport. In the November 1964 election, Governor Edgar's Republican Party won control of both houses of the Illinois Legislature. The polls had barely closed when GOP leaders expressed their intent to take over O'Hare International Airport by creating a regional airport authority.

Mayor Daley and Chicago's City Council were outraged. Perhaps the Republicans also wanted to snatch Chicago's water purification plant, the mayor suggested.

"It will be a no-frills, user-friendly terminal," said then-Aviation Commissioner Mosena, "designed to better meet the needs of the traveling public and to be affordable to the low-cost carriers."

Architects were retained to design a blueprint for the new terminal, with construction scheduled for completion around the year 2000. The basic plans were barely complete when the project was temporarily put on hold.

Governor Edgar had been pushing for a $5.1 billion airport, the third in the Chicago area — with another $1 billion for infrastructure — in the tiny rural community of Peotone, 35 miles south of downtown Chicago. The governor

In April 1995, the GOP threat to seize O'Hare suddenly materialized. Republicans declared they would submit proposed legislation for a new regional airport authority to the General Assembly — and even revealed the date they would introduce the bill in the State Capitol. At City Hall, the midnight oil was not only burning — it was smoking.

Finally, on a Saturday morning just four days before the takeover bill was to be introduced in the legislature, a news conference was scheduled at the Gary, Indiana, airport. Mayor Daley joined Indiana Governor Evan Bayh and Gary officials to sign documents creating a Chicago-Gary regional airport authority. If the Republicans still harbored dreams of a regional airport authority, they would have to annex the state of Indiana. The grand plan to seize control of Chicago's airports died on the tarmac of Gary Airport.

As the next century approaches, Chicago's airport system faces more than political challenges. With deregulation, lower air fares, and more competition, the complexion of aviation changes from day to day, and airports, like other businesses, are competing for travelers. With its resources, its commitment to service and security, and its long-range strategic planning, O'Hare stands as a beacon in a thriving region, beckoning travelers to its world-class facility.

BUCKINGHAM FOUNTAIN; PHOTO BY JAMES BLANK©

PART TWO

Chicago Enterprises

Welcome To Chicago's O'Hare

rport **Richard M. Daley, Mayor**

AIRLINE INDUSTRY

THE

CHAPTER SIX

United Airlines

"Chicago's hometown airline" soars as a national and international aviation leader

To the international airline network, United Airlines is the world's largest carrier; a mega giant whose fleet of more than 550 jet planes spans the globe, serving more than 100 U.S. and 40 international airports in 30 countries.

But to the city of Chicago, where it has its headquarters and main hub, United is an economic marvel, employing nearly 16,000 area residents, and generating $673 million in payroll and almost $100 million in landing and airport rental fees annually.

A star tenant of O'Hare International Airport, United, along with its regional airline affiliate United Express, serves nearly half of the incoming and outbound passengers, offer-

ing more flights than any other airline at the airfield — in excess of 500 daily departures. Therefore, when United

TOP PHOTO: IN TODAY'S BUSINESS WORLD, EVERY SECOND COUNTS, AND UNITED ACCOMMODATES ITS PASSENGERS ACCORDINGLY. ABOVE: THE BOEING 777 IS UNITED'S LARGEST, MOST INNOVATIVE TWIN-ENGINE JUMBO JET.

identifies itself in its Chicago-area advertisements as "Chicago's hometown airline," it is not exaggerating.

United's roots can be traced back to Varney Airlines, established in Pasco, Washington, in 1926. Varney, along with Pacific Air Transport, National Air Transport and Boeing Air Transport, merged to form United Air Lines in the early 1930s. The newly formed company began offering the nation's first coast-to-coast airline service.

In 1934, United's manufacturing and transportation divisions separated. Bill Patterson, United's future president, decided that Chicago would be the best place for the fledgling carrier to sprout its wings. In an interview with the *Chicago Tribune* several years after the move, Patterson, who served as United's chairman until 1963, explained why he brought the airline to the Windy City.

"It seemed to me that Chicago would be a more representative center for a national organization than any other city," he said. "We've never regretted our choice."

Neither, for that matter, has Chicago.

United began at O'Hare with only 10 inbound and 10 outbound flights a day, but the numbers climbed quickly as airlines increasingly transferred their commercial flight operations from Midway Airport in the late 1950s. In 1962, United moved its corporate headquarters from Midway to a sprawling facility about five miles northwest of O'Hare, its new base of operations.

As its O'Hare operations continued to expand, the airline soon needed more terminal space at the airport. In the 1980s, it undertook construction of a new $556.5 million passenger terminal. This 20-acre aluminum-and-glass structure, with its two 1,500-foot-long concourses, is among the most spectacular and functional airline terminals in the world.

Opened in August 1987, the terminal includes 52 departure gates; 56 flow-through ticket counters for passenger check-in; computerized digital signs; 10 flow-through security checkpoints; a state-of-the-art baggage system with capacity for 480 pieces of baggage per minute; a full-service restaurant; and dozens of shops, lounges, and eateries. Perhaps the most amazing sight is the 744-foot-long passageway between the terminal's main and satellite concourses, where moving sidewalks

carry passengers through a tunnel that features a dazzling overhead neon-light sculpture synchronized to change colors to background music.

Today at O'Hare, United hosts nearly 15 million passengers a year and offers nonstop flights to 88 U.S. cities and seven international metropolitan areas, including Mexico City, London, Paris, Frankfurt, Vancouver, Toronto, San Juan, and Tokyo. System wide, United serves about 80 million passengers a year, and it employs approximately 80,000 people.

United is unique in that it is an employee-owned airline. In fact, it is the largest and, to date, most successful employee-owned company in the nation. In 1994, airline employees purchased a majority stake in the carrier and its holding company, UAL Corp., granting the airline $4.9 billion in work-rule changes and wage and benefit cuts in exchange for 55 percent of its stock. The employee buyout has "added a new spirit" at United, according to Gerald Greenwald, the airline's current chairman and CEO. It has also significantly improved the airline's profitability over the last three years.

United Airlines will continue to be a major presence on the national and international aviation scene for years to come, but among Chicagoans it will always affectionately be referred to as "Chicago's hometown airline."

ABOVE: UNITED'S O'HARE TERMINAL FEATURES A FUTURISTIC PASSAGEWAY WITH A SPECTACULAR OVERHEAD NEON-LIGHT SCULPTURE. LEFT: UNITED IS RENOWNED FOR ITS EXCEPTIONAL IN-FLIGHT CUSTOMER SERVICE.

American Airlines

The airline that "means business" provides unparalleled passenger service and comfort

In Chicago, as in other major cities across the country, "American Means Business." This is not only a corporate slogan, but an expression of American's commitment to service. American, together with its regional airline partner, American Eagle, offers nearly 500 flights each business day from O'Hare International Airport. With a modern 700,000-square-foot terminal, 47 departure gates, 170 aircraft assigned to the city's principal airfield, and 11,000 Chicago-based employees, American is, indeed, big business in the Windy City.

Its economic impact on Chicago and the value of the service it provides to business and leisure travelers in the area are monumental. Moreover, American's huge route network links Chicago with nearly 260 cities in more than 45 countries around the world, helping make the Windy City one of the nation's principal air transportation hubs. Chances are that American Airlines, its regional associate American Eagle, or one of its code-sharing air-line partners strategically located around the globe can take you to any destination in the world from Chicago.

American has one of the most extensive route networks of any airline in the world, offering approximately 4,000 flights a day from all the destinations it serves. From Chicago alone, the carrier serves 107 cities, with non-stop flights to more than 70 of them. From O'Hare, American flies to almost 20 foreign countries. Since 1982, Chicago has been American's mid-continent "GatewAAy to Europe." Today, American is the largest international carrier at O'Hare, with daily nonstop service to 10 cities in eight European countries.

At O'Hare, American boasts the world's largest VIP lounge, offering a corporate atmosphere enhanced by club amenities. The 33,000-square-foot Admirals Club features everything a business traveler might need … even showers. The Executive Center has 19 specially designed conference rooms with audio/video equipment, presentation boards, speakerphones, and controlled lighting. The rooms can function as branch offices, meeting rooms, or presentation areas.

ABOVE: AMERICAN AND AMERICAN EAGLE TOGETHER OFFER NEARLY 500 DAILY DEPARTURES EVERY BUSINESS DAY FROM O'HARE INTERNATIONAL AIRPORT. RIGHT: AMERICAN BOASTS A FLEET OF MORE THAN 650 JET PLANES.

Because of American's tremendous reach, millions of air travelers in Chicago and worldwide enjoy convenient service to the most prominent business and leisure centers in the United States, Canada, Mexico, the Caribbean, Latin America, Europe, and Japan. Last year, American carried more than 80 million passengers worldwide. That translates into an average of more than 220,000 customers a day and more than 1.5 million passengers a week.

Although originally based in New York City, American has been an important entity in Chicago for many years — first at Midway Airport, then at O'Hare, from the time it opened in 1955. In fact, the first regularly scheduled flight into O'Hare was an American Airlines flight from Detroit on October 30, 1955.

American Airlines began with 12 scheduled flights per day at O'Hare. By 1969, however, the number of flights increased to more than 300. Today, the airline is one of the most prominent tenants at the world's busiest airport. O'Hare is American's second-largest hub after Dallas-Fort Worth International Airport, American's home base.

American's roots can be traced back to the 1920s. In 1929, Aviation Corp., a New York holding firm, was created to oversee Fairchild Aviation Corp.'s airplane manufacturing activities and the operations of 85 small regional airlines nationwide. The following year, Aviation Corp. consolidated the smaller carriers into one large transcontinental airline, American Airways. In 1934, the aircraft manufacturing operation and airline were split into two separate companies and, as a result, American Airways became American Airlines.

This newly organized carrier rapidly rose to the top of the list of U.S. carriers. Under the chairmanship of the legendary C.R. Smith, American became the country's leading airline by the late 1930s.

American began flexing its wings internationally in 1971, when it bought Trans Caribbean Airlines. After the deregulation of the U.S. airline industry in the late 1970s, it quickly expanded its reach around the world, establishing itself as a global giant. With the guidance of Robert L. Crandall, its current chairman, American Airlines and its parent company, AMR Corp., ventured across the Atlantic,

organizing nonstop service to Europe and added flights to Tokyo and Madrid. In 1991, American acquired TWA's routes from the U.S. to London's Heathrow Airport, the main gateway to European destinations.

Since its inception, American has proven itself to be one of the most innovative U.S. carriers. In the 1930s, it introduced the Douglas DC-3 into service and became the first commercial airline to operate on passenger revenues alone. American was the first to launch a frequent flier reward program. It also presented SABRE, the industry's first automated reservations system.

American Airlines, however, considers its greatest accomplishment to be its long-standing reputation for outstanding passenger service and comfort. American Airlines has always strived to be the very best.

TOP PHOTO: AMERICAN PRIDES ITSELF ON CONSISTENTLY EXCELLENT CUSTOMER SERVICE. ABOVE: AMERICAN'S STATE-OF-THE-ART TERMINAL AT O'HARE INTERNATIONAL IS BOTH HIGHLY FUNCTIONAL AND AESTHETICALLY PLEASING.

Swissair

Honored worldwide as first in its class for exceptional first- and business-class service

More than 2,200 frequent fliers from 10 European countries praised Swissair as — "the best airline in Europe" — in a 1995 poll by Total Research, an independent British institute, for the annual Airtrack survey. It was the second year in a row that the Swiss national carrier had been named Europe's top passenger carrier in this prestigious survey.

In the 1995 poll, Swissair placed first in the individual categories of overall satisfaction, punctuality, leg room, seat comfort, friendliness of staff, quality, and in-flight catering. Such accolades from veteran airline passengers are not new to Swissair. Since its inception in 1931, the carrier, which flies to Switzerland six times a week from Chicago's O'Hare International Airport, has accumulated dozens of awards for the quality of its product and services.

Other recent honors bestowed on the carrier include being named "the most punctual airline" in a poll among readers of Great Britain's respected *Business Traveller* magazine; "the best international carrier" in a poll conducted by *Incentive,* a U.S.-based trade magazine; "best airline" by the readers of France's *Conde Nast Traveler* magazine; and "best airline worldwide" in a poll of top travel trade managers undertaken by Germany's *Holiday Magazine.*

What accounts for Swissair's international award-winning ways? The answer, Swissair officials say, is simple — understanding and fulfilling the needs and wishes of passengers. The airline openly encourages its travelers to express their needs, preferences, and comments.

"This communication is essential to our customers' satisfaction, and that satisfaction is vital to our corporate success," says Otto Loepfe, president and CEO of the Swissair Group, the parent company of Swissair. "Our customers take center stage in everything we devise and do," Loepfe adds. "At Swissair, however, we don't just aim to meet our customers' needs, we strive to exceed them." For example, in response to the need of business travelers to keep in touch with associates while traveling, Swissair recently installed in-flight telephones on its fleet of Boeing 747, McDonnell Douglas MD-11, and Airbus 320 jets, thus allowing passengers to make telephone calls on all overseas flights and on short-haul flights within Europe.

Another recent innovation resulting from passenger suggestions is the inclusion of Swissair flight and service information on the Internet. The information provided includes a list of flight connections between the 13,000 city pairs served by Swissair and by Crossair, its regional European carrier. The flight schedules of Swissair's code-sharing partners — Delta Air Lines, USAir, Air Canada, and Singapore Airlines, among others — are also included. Swissair's World Wide Web address is http://www. swissair.com. The site allows travelers

RIGHT AND FACING PAGE: WITH A FLEET OF MORE THAN 60 JET AIRCRAFT (PICTURED ARE SWISSAIR'S MCDONNELL DOUGLAS MD 11S) AND A WORK FORCE EXCEEDING 16,000 PEOPLE WORLDWIDE, SWISSAIR SERVES MORE THAN 115 DESTINATIONS AROUND THE WORLD. FOR FLIGHTS INTO AND OUT OF THE U.S., SWISSAIR OFFERS HUBS IN CHICAGO AS WELL AS LOS ANGELES, ATLANTA, BOSTON, PHILADELPHIA, NEW YORK, AND WASHINGTON, D.C.

to arrange their flight schedule and timetable and to learn about the cities and airports they plan to visit.

When it comes to quality service, few airlines can match Swissair, which takes notice of not only mainstream concerns but also small details. Meals aboard a Swissair flight, for instance, are tailored to fit each passenger's preferences. In business class on overseas flights, passengers can order a buffet (a cold dish served just after takeoff) as an alternative to the standard full-course three-dish meal so they can have more time to nap or relax during the flight.

In first class on overnight flights, flight attendants will, upon request, turn a passenger's seat into a real bed, complete with duvet and pillow. And when passengers arrive at Swissair's Zurich hub, they can take advantage of the airline's new Allegra Arrival Lounge, which is equipped with showers, dayrooms, a cafe, a wide range of newspapers, and the usual communications facilities.

At Swissair, quality service goes far beyond fulfilling customers' needs and preferences. As a global corporate citizen, this Swiss airline is deeply concerned about the fate of all mankind, especially with respect to the environment. As part of its efforts to ensure that future generations will be able to breathe clean air, Swissair has committed itself to minimizing air and noise pollutants associated with airline operations. For example, the carrier has made a point of acquiring fuel-efficient, low-noise aircraft types. As a result, Swissair has one of the world's youngest and most advanced aircraft fleets. The average age of its aircraft is less than seven years.

Among other things, the airline also has invested heavily in sound-muffling devices for its aircraft engine test stands, it operates a wastewater recycling plant, and it has begun switching its diesel- and gasoline-powered ground vehicles to electric power. It even separates the garbage accumulated on its flights into various

categories — aluminum, glass, tin, plastic — and sends it to recycling plants in Zurich and Geneva.

Furthermore, Swissair has committed itself to expanding its airline at a moderate pace to ensure that Switzerland's international airports won't become overly congested.

With a fleet of more than 60 jet aircraft and a work force exceeding 16,000 people worldwide, Swissair serves more than 115 destinations around the world. From the U.S., global destinations can be reached via Swissair's hubs in Geneva and Zurich. In addition to Chicago, Swissair flies into and out of the United States from Atlanta, Los Angeles, New York, Philadelphia, Boston, and Washington, D.C.

An ever-increasing number of travelers are becoming acquainted with Swissair's award-winning service. In 1995 alone, the carrier flew more than 8.6 million passengers. That's roughly three times the population of the city of Chicago.

Hudson General LLC

Providing high-quality aviation services to O'Hare and other North American airports

It can be said that Hudson General LLC does everything for airlines, airport operators, and the general aviation community but fly their airplanes.

Based in Great Neck, New York, Hudson General, with annual revenues in excess of $150 million, is a company whose primary business is providing a broad array of services to airport operators and airlines at airports throughout the United States and Canada.

With a work force of more than 3,800 employees, the company provides ground handling services for domestic and international airlines, as well as for corporate and private aircraft owners, at 26 airports across North America.

ABOVE AND RIGHT: HUDSON GENERAL, IN BUSINESS FOR MORE THAN 35 YEARS, HAS BEEN PROVIDING AVIATION SERVICES AT O'HARE INTERNATIONAL FOR MORE THAN A QUARTER OF A CENTURY.

Founded in 1961, Hudson General was principally a finance company with holdings in such diverse industries as real estate, computers, shoe machinery, and all modes of transportation. The firm provided financing services to North American-based aviation service companies in the mid-1960s. Over time, Hudson General acquired ownership and management of these entities.

By the late 1970s, Hudson General altered its business direction, focusing all its efforts on aviation services, with the exception of one real estate project in Hawaii which it still maintains. Over the next few years, it divested itself of all other investments.

The company's focus and commitment to the aviation industry proved to be very fortuitous, as the United States deregulated its commercial aviation industry, resulting in growth of tremendous proportions. Start-up carriers sought out qualified companies to service their aircraft, and Hudson General took this opportunity to expand its core businesses. The company also added many related services in order to develop a "one-stop shop" for its customer base.

As global deregulation and liberalization spread, Hudson General made a strategic decision to stay within the geographic boundaries of the U.S. and Canada, even though many of its North American competitors attempted to become worldwide aviation service providers. Company officials feel Hudson General has benefited from its competitors' actions. At the same time, its own national business perimeters are continuously expanding.

Hudson General's business philosophy is simple and straightforward — deliver a superior service product to the customer at a fair and reasonable price. The company takes great pride in the fact that many of its contracts have been in place for more than 30 consecutive years. Customer loyalty of this order in a highly competitive industry is quite an accomplishment.

Hudson General also prides itself on the continuity of its management. The company's founder, Chief Executive Officer and Chairman Jay B. Langner, has held this position since the firm's inception. The company

actively practices and encourages a policy of promotion from within. In an era of corporate downsizing, this policy is, indeed, rare. It has proven to be very beneficial for Hudson General and its customers.

Hudson General's scope of services includes: passenger assistance, ramp handling, aircraft maintenance, airport snow removal and deicing, glycol recovery, fuel services management, cargo warehousing, and ground transportation.

Currently, Hudson General employs approximately 325 people at O'Hare International Airport, providing service for more than 150 aircraft per day. The company delivers approximately 15 million gallons of jet fuel monthly to many of the interna-

tional and domestic passenger and cargo air carriers serving O'Hare. The firm also provides snow removal at most of the airport's passenger terminals, as well as airline cargo and hangar areas. To serve the airport and its airline tenants, including the airport's largest carriers, American Airlines and United Airlines, Hudson General utilizes more than 200 pieces of state-of-the-art snow removal equipment.

Because the aviation business is growing, and airlines and airport operators are increasingly relinquishing service functions to independent firms, the future of aviation companies such as Hudson General looks very bright.

"Hudson General continuously investigates expansion of its core busi-

nesses and locations while maintaining a high quality of service," says Jim Rhea, General Manager at Hudson General LLC.

In fact, in May 1996, Hudson General Corporation sold to Lufthansa Airport and Group Services (LAGS) 26 percent of its aviation services business. This relationship will provide Hudson General LLC with direct access to the worldwide network of aviation partners and customers of LAGS. It will also create opportunities for Hudson General beyond its current geographic boundaries.

Hudson General LLC accepts these challenges and has developed a niche within the Chicago community. For additional information on Hudson General LLC, call (847) 298-6140.

ABOVE: HUDSON GENERAL PROVIDES GROUND HANDLING SERVICES FOR DOMESTIC AND INTERNATIONAL AIRLINES AND FOR CORPORATE AND PRIVATE AIRCRAFT OWNERS AT 26 NORTH AMERICAN AIRPORTS. LEFT: THE COMPANY PROVIDES SNOW REMOVAL SERVICES AT SEVERAL AIRPORTS IN THE NORTHEAST AND MIDWEST, INCLUDING O'HARE INTERNATIONAL AIRPORT.

Korean Air

A higher level of gracious first-, business-, and economy-class passenger service

A irlines recognized by travelers as being among the world's leading carriers usually require 50 or more years in the business to achieve their lofty reputations. Korean Air did it before the company even celebrated its 25th anniversary in 1994.

The reason this international carrier has blossomed so quickly into a premier airline can be summed up in two words — passenger service.

"No other words have been so important in shaping our goals and guiding our energies in all aspects of the airline business," says Choong

TOP AND ABOVE RIGHT: KOREAN AIR STRIVES TO MAKE ITS PASSENGERS FEEL LIKE ROYALTY. EACH PASSENGER IN EACH CLASS OF SEATING IS PROVIDED WITH TEMPTING FARE, MUSIC, IN-FLIGHT MOVIES, AND THE GRACIOUS SERVICE FOR WHICH THIS AIRLINE IS KNOWN.

Hoon Cho, Korean Air's chairman and CEO. "To Korean Air, passenger service, which we sum up as a customer-focused mind-set and a dedication to serving the customer, is the embodiment of quality. Without this focus, our identity as an airline would lose all value. For this reason, Korean Air has been relentless in its drive to reach higher and higher levels of passenger service excellence."

Indeed, from its humble beginnings in 1969, when it succeeded the state-owned Korean Airline Corporation, Korean Air has made a point of trying to make each and every one of its passengers feel like royalty.

Today, the array of amenities provided to passengers before and after boarding one of Korean Air's more than 100 Boeing, McDonnell Douglas, Airbus, and Fokker jets can only be described as regal.

First-class passengers experience the height of gracious service from the moment they step up to one of Korean Air's special first-class check-in counters at one of the two dozen domestic airports or more than 60 overseas airfields served by the carrier, including Chicago O'Hare International Airport.

Once their tickets are processed and bags are checked in, first-class passengers are directed to the airline's special "Morning Calm" lounge, where they can relax with a soft drink and a newspaper or magazine in a comfortable and quiet atmosphere until takeoff.

Inside one of Korean Air's first-class cabins — referred to by Korean Air personnel as "flying guest rooms" — each passenger is greeted by a flight attendant assigned to that section. The attendants, who often are dressed in colorful native Korean dress, then escort each passenger to one of the cabin's seats, which are designed so that a traveler can recline up to a 60-degree pitch and stretch his or her legs fully onto a footrest attached to each seat. Because the legroom between each seat is a generous 62 inches, even travelers con-

siderably taller than six feet can fly in complete comfort.

Awaiting first-class passengers once their Korean Air jet is off the ground is a fine selection of superb wines, cocktails, champagne, appetizers (including caviar or pate de foie gras), and meals that include beef dishes, specially prepared fish entrees, and traditional Korean dishes.

"In fact, our first-class cabin rates as the world's finest restaurant in the air," the airline's chairman points out.

As an added touch, Korean Air serves its first-class travelers a portion of fresh ginseng, a tonic herb native to Korea. The ginseng, mixed with honey, banishes fatigue on long flights, according to traditional wisdom and Korean Air officials.

Business-class travelers can also look forward to special check-in counter service at the airport and plenty of seating comfort aboard a Korean Air flight. Seats in the business section — or Prestige Class, as

Korean Air calls it — allow travelers to recline at a 38-degree pitch. Furthermore, the 41 inches of space between seats is as wide or wider than in the first-class sections of most other airlines.

Unlike most airlines, the business-class section aboard Korean Air is in the front of the airplane. That's where most of the other airlines locate their first-class section. This way, business people on a tight schedule can get off the airplane quickly once they reach one of the more than 70 worldwide cities served by Korean Air.

Although economy-class passengers may not have all of the seating comforts enjoyed by first- and busi-

ness-class passengers, each is treated as a special guest and provided with many of the same first-class comforts, including in-flight movies, music, and food that embody the rich cultural heritage of the Korean people. Most importantly, economy-class passengers experience the same gracious hospitality that is accorded to passengers in the two upscale-class cabins.

One reason why Korean Air provides its passengers with traditional Korean hospitality and an array of top-notch amenities is that doing so makes good business sense. A more important reason, however, is that Korean Air managers and employees value and apply the qualities of diligence and spirit of service.

Cho notes, "It is these qualities, evident in our country's 5,000-year history and embodied in our staff, that will ensure Korean Air will become the very best in the world in the twenty-first century."

ABOVE AND LEFT: IN LESS THAN 30 YEARS OF ITS EXISTENCE, KOREAN AIR HAS RISEN AS ONE OF THE WORLD'S PREMIER AIRLINES. A COMPANY-WIDE COMMITMENT TO SAFETY, SERVICE, AND OVERALL EXCELLENCE HAS CONTRIBUTED TO THIS AIRLINE'S SUCCESS.

China Eastern Airlines

China's premier domestic airline now circles the globe with its international routes

The opportunities for Chicago residents traveling to China on business or for a vacation were significantly enhanced in April 1993, thanks to China Eastern Airlines.

That's when this Chinese air carrier launched two passenger flights a week — on Thursdays and Sundays — from Chicago O'Hare International Airport to Shanghai and Beijing via Seattle.

Since the inception of these flights, thousands of Chicago residents and people from throughout the Midwest have availed themselves of the chance to visit one of the largest, most exotic, and culturally rich nations in the world.

Once a passenger reaches Shanghai or Beijing aboard China Eastern, the airline can put him or her on a connecting China Eastern flight to any of 50 cities within China as well as to the nearby city of Hong Kong and state of Singapore.

Although China Eastern may not yet be a household name among U.S. air travelers and freight shippers, the carrier has a history in China

RIGHT: EXCEPTIONAL SERVICE IS EXTENDED TO THE MORE THAN SIX MILLION PASSENGERS THAT FLY YEARLY WITH CHINA EASTERN AIRLINES. THIS AIRLINE, ONE OF THE WORLD'S MOST PROFITABLE, FLIES TO AND FROM THE U.S., HONG KONG, SINGAPORE, JAPAN, SOUTH KOREA, THAILAND, BELGIUM, AND SPAIN, IN ADDITION TO ITS 50 DOMESTIC ROUTES WITHIN CHINA.

that dates back nearly 50 years — longer than most U.S. carriers have been in existence. It was established by the Chinese government as China's premier domestic airline in 1949 and was operated under the direction of the government's aviation authority until 1988.

As a result of economic decentralization reforms undertaken by the Chinese government in 1988, China Eastern Airlines became one of about 50 large Chinese businesses to be granted a significant amount of autonomy from government control to see if they could operate successfully as independent business entities in the world's expanding free-market economy. To date, China Eastern is showing that, at least in the airline business, the experiment is paying off.

With its fleet of nearly 50 jets, including McDonnell-Douglas MD-11s and MD-82s, Airbus 340s and Airbus 300s, and Fokker 100s, China Eastern Airlines' business is skyrocketing. In fact, in 1993 it became the 11th most profitable airline in the world. More recently, plans were laid

for the carrier's parent company, China Eastern Air Group, to make an initial public stock offering on one or more of the world's stock exchanges.

Today, China Eastern flies nearly six million passengers annually and carries about 180 thousand tons of cargo a year. In addition to its 50 domestic routes within China and its flights to and from the U.S., Hong Kong, and Singapore, it flies to Belgium, Spain, Japan, South Korea, and Thailand. It also maintains reservations and business offices throughout the world, including one on Chicago's North Michigan Avenue.

The goal of China Eastern's managers is to grow their enterprise as a successful company that competes with any aviation firm in the world. Based on China Eastern's track record, it appears that the company continues to more than meet that goal.

LOT Polish Airlines

The preferred alternative for travelers to Europe has been serving O'Hare since 1973

Once regarded simply as a shuttle service between the United States and Poland, LOT Polish Airlines has emerged as the preferred alternative to Europe for many business and vacation travelers.

With U.S. offices in New York, Chicago, Los Angeles, and Miami, and a Canadian office in Toronto, LOT has been an international passenger carrier since before World War II. While it has undergone an impressive overhaul of its fleet and facilities over the last several years, it continues to retain its uncompromising dedication to customer service.

With the switch from its former fleet of Soviet-made Aeroflot planes to modern Boeing 767 jets, LOT today boasts the youngest fleet in the airline industry. Its Boeing 767 aircraft have been in service, on average, for only three years. Now this airline has the aircraft to match its reputation in superior customer service, according to Mark Kawczynski, LOT's Midwest general manager.

"The increase in business as a result of the new aircraft has been dramatic," says Kawczynski. "People just didn't trust the Russian planes."

LOT's annual average passenger load per flight has risen to an enviable 70 percent since the addition of the new Boeing aircraft. During the holiday season, the passenger capacity on flights usually reaches 100 percent. In fact, most holiday-period flights are booked solid by September, Kawczynski notes.

The new, more efficient fleet of U.S.-made Boeing airplanes has also allowed LOT to significantly reduce its operating costs. "The Boeing 767 seats 60 more passengers and requires 40 percent less fuel per flight," says Kawczynski. "In addition, the Russian planes required a crew of five, whereas now we need only two people."

LOT has been a fixture at O'Hare International Airport since 1973, serving business and leisure travelers alike. It has been especially important as a service provider to the metropolitan area's large Polish population, the largest in the world outside of Warsaw, Poland's capital. For recent immigrants and first-genera-

tion Polish Americans it has been a lifeline to families and friends in Poland. For other Polish Americans, it offers the opportunity to visit and become acquainted with the nation and culture from which their roots spring.

Today, LOT's service area has expanded far beyond Poland. Its market now includes almost all European countries, and several destinations in the Middle and Far East. On transatlantic routes to the United States, LOT cooperates closely with American Airlines.

In Chicago, LOT Polish Airlines' reservations and information office is located at 333 North Michigan Avenue, Suite 921. Reservations on LOT flights can also be made through one's local travel agent.

ABOVE: WITH ITS NEW BOEING 767 JETS, LOT POLISH AIRLINES BOASTS THE YOUNGEST FLEET OF PLANES IN THE INDUSTRY. LEFT: LOT'S OFFICIALS ATTRIBUTE THE AIRLINE'S SUCCESS TO ITS STATE-OF-THE-ART IN-FLIGHT AMENITIES AND OUTSTANDING CUSTOMER SERVICE.

British Airways

The king of international air routes provides top-notch service and amenities

Britannia may no longer rule the waves, but its flagship airline — British Airways — is king of the international air routes that circle the globe.

While other air carriers may operate more flights and carry more passengers because of their huge domestic route networks, British Airways leads the pack when it comes to international flying.

With its fleet of 295 white and navy-blue aircraft, the British carrier transports more than 36 million passengers annually to more than 160 destinations in more than 80 countries. And through alliances with other airlines and part ownership of carriers such as USAir, Qantas, TAT European Airlines, and Deutsche BA, British Airways reaches more than 400 destinations worldwide.

"It's the modern-day equivalent of Pan American World Airways," a top executive at one of British Airways' chief rivals in the transatlantic market freely acknowledges. "It has the global reach and reputation for first-rate service that Pan Am had in its heyday."

Much of British Airways' success is attributed to its marketing strategy. Unlike most of its peers in the airline industry, this airline has steered clear of offering cheap fares to attract passengers. Instead, British Airways has made a point of reaching upscale international business travelers and then attracting and keeping their patronage by providing top-notch service.

Indeed, British Airways provides its passengers with a stream of ser-

vices and amenities — everything from individual seat-back high-definition video screens to lip balm and eye compresses (to help fight flight fatigue). And the in-flight food service provided would put many upscale restaurants around the world to shame.

This marketing tactic has proved to be very successful. Sir Colin Marshall, the airline's chairman, estimates that about 80 percent of the carrier's revenues are generated from passengers who purchase tickets for first-class and business-class seats. Most importantly, the carrier continually turns a profit. In fact, while most U.S. and European airlines lost hundreds of millions of dollars during the recessionary early 1990s, British Airways cruised comfortably in the black.

British Airways' huge Boeing 747 and 767 aircraft are a familiar sight at Chicago O'Hare International Airport. British Airways flies twice daily from O'Hare to London's Heathrow Airport from April 1 until the end of

October, and once a day between November 1 and the end of March. Approximately 1,400 passengers depart from or arrive daily to Chicago aboard British Airways' aircraft.

In fact, British Airways has been serving Chicago since 1954, before O'Hare International became the city's primary airport. In 1956, when most commercial airlines transferred their operations to O'Hare from Chicago's Midway Airport, British Airways was the first carrier from overseas to fly in and out of the new facility.

ABOVE: BRITISH AIRWAYS' BOEING 747 AIRCRAFT ARE A FAMILIAR SIGHT AT CHICAGO O'HARE INTERNATIONAL AIRPORT. THIS DISTINCTIVE FLEET OF 295 WHITE AND NAVY-BLUE AIRCRAFT CARRIERS TRANSPORTS MORE THAN 36 MILLION PASSENGERS ANNUALLY TO MORE THAN 160 DESTINATIONS IN MORE THAN 80 COUNTRIES.

Airport & Airline Services

CHAPTER SEVEN

The University of Illinois at Chicago Medical Center

World-class medicine at world's busiest airport

or many years at many airports around the country, a traveler in physical distress could find little more than Band-Aid, Pepto-Bismol, and aspirin in one of those convenience shops scattered throughout airport terminals.

That's still the case in a lot of U.S. airports, but not at Chicago O'Hare International Airport, where a full-service clinic — operated by the University of Illinois at Chicago (UIC) Medical Center — has been dispensing medical care at Terminal 2 since November 1995.

In 1994, realizing the benefits of having doctors available every day at the world's busiest airport, the City of Chicago's Department of Aviation asked health care providers to submit bids for operating such a facility. The

UIC Medical Center responded with an offer that city officials could hardly refuse: It agreed to establish and run the clinic at no extra cost to the city.

Given the fact that O'Hare International Airport is the size of some cities, it made sense to have "a doctor in town," said UIC Medical Center officials.

The 1,600-square-foot facility provides medical care for those among the 200,000 passengers using the airport daily who need immediate emergency medical care or simply require treatment or advice for a minor medical problem. The clinic is open daily, 6 a.m. to midnight, and is staffed by UIC Medical Center emergency medicine physicians, occupational medicine physicians, residents, nurses, X-ray technicians, and administrative support staff, all of whom also care for airline crews and the airport's 50,000 employees.

"We wear two hats here," says a spokesperson for the O'Hare clinic.

"The airport medical center is set up as a mini-emergency room, but it also functions as an occupational health center."

Indeed, on a typical day, the clinic provides both levels of care. Recently, within an 18-hour period, doctors staffing the clinic provided emergency treatment to a flight attendant, suspected of having a diseased gall bladder, before transferring her to a nearby hospital. Later that same day, the staff did an EKG on a passenger who had experienced mild chest pains during a flight from

LEFT: THE UIC MEDICAL CENTER, A FULL-SERVICE CLINIC, IS LOCATED AT O'HARE INTERNATIONAL'S TERMINAL 2. ABOVE: THE MEDICAL CENTER PROVIDES EMPLOYEE, OCCUPATIONAL HEALTH, AND EMERGENCY MEDICAL CARE. *BOTH PHOTOS BY ROBERTA DUPUIS-DEVLIN/ UNIVERSITY OF ILLINOIS AT CHICAGO*

London, treated an airline pilot for strep throat, X-rayed the arm of an airport ramp worker who took a nasty fall on the job, and gave an airport maintenance employee the physical he needed in order to return to work following a long illness. In between, the staff explained to a foreign visitor how to obtain a refill for the prescription medication he needed, and treated a handful of passengers and airport employees for a variety of minor medical problems ranging from air sickness to a scraped elbow.

"The UIC Medical Center at O'Hare is capable of providing the

care that airline passengers, airline personnel, and airport employees need, whether it is nonemergency or emergency care, whether it is a minor or more serious medical problem," says the UIC Medical Center spokesperson.

The clinic also provides job-related physicals and follow-up exams to airline personnel, airport workers, and employees working for firms near O'Hare International. The center even has staff capable of conducting health hazard screenings and handicap accessibility evaluations for airlines and other airport employers.

Perhaps the clinic's most important attribute, however, is its affiliation with the University of Illinois at Chicago Colleges of Medicine, Nursing and Pharmacy, and the UIC Medical Center, which comprises a 450-bed hospital and 100 diagnostic and specialty clinics. The UIC Medical Center is located just west of downtown Chicago.

Should the Medical Center at O'Hare be faced with a special or unusual medical problem or emergency, it has instant access to the expertise of the medical professionals at the medical school and, if necessary, can admit patients to the university's hospital or one of its diagnostic or specialty clinics. This affiliation can be especially important to foreign visitors and U.S. travelers who may be unfamiliar with Chicago and suddenly find themselves in need of immediate medical attention.

The clinic's affiliation with such a culturally and academically diverse institution as the University of Illinois at Chicago also assures foreign visitors to the airport that their medical problems will be understood within the context of their cultural or ethnic background, even if they have difficulty communicating in English.

"Through the university and the City of Chicago, one of the world's truly great cosmopolitan and ethnically diverse cities, we have the ability to provide translators for virtually every patient from abroad who visits the O'Hare Medical Center," says the spokesperson for the UIC Medical Center.

TOP PHOTO: THE UNIVERSITY OF ILLINOIS AT CHICAGO IS THE LARGEST INSTITUTION OF HIGHER LEARNING IN THE CHICAGO AREA. ABOVE LEFT: SHOWN IS THE MAIN CAMPUS OF THE UIC MEDICAL CENTER. *BOTH PHOTOS BY ROBERTA DUPUIS-DEVLIN/UNIVERSITY OF ILLINOIS AT CHICAGO*

O'Hare Hilton Hotel

Conveniently located at O'Hare International; well suited for business travelers

The O'Hare Hilton is unique among the many hotels surrounding Chicago O'Hare International Airport — it is the only one located inside the grounds of the world's busiest airfield.

The 858-room, 10-story structure is centered among O'Hare's four main domestic airline terminals. It's just a short walk, via an underground pedestrian walkway, from the ticket counters and gates of all the domestic airlines serving the airfield. And the hotel is only a short airport-train ride away from O'Hare's new International Terminal.

Completed in 1974 and owned by Hilton since 1991, the O'Hare Hilton underwent a $42 million renovation in 1992 and has recently added a full-service health club that includes simulated golf.

Because of its unique location at the very crossroads of the nation's air routes, the O'Hare Hilton is a convenient meeting place for regional, national, and even international business conferences.

"A large number of national and international corporations and associations like to hold their meetings here because of the hotel's convenient location on the airport property," says Ken Smith, general manager of the O'Hare Hilton. "Once they arrive at the airport, they don't have to deal with traffic or the weather."

With 42 meeting rooms of varying size, plus nine banquet-meeting rooms and three ballrooms, the O'Hare Hilton Hotel can accommodate a business gathering of just about any configuration.

The Hilton's guest rooms, most of which offer a breathtaking view of aircraft arrivals and departures, are equipped with the business traveler in mind. Each is outfitted with an executive desk and two telephones with data port and voice mail features. More than half the rooms also have a fax machine.

Besides traditional rooms, the Hilton also has 31 suites, including two deluxe executive suites on the hotel's top floor that have space for intimate receptions and/or gatherings.

As for food, the hotel has two dining establishments located off its spacious lobby. Andiamo offers family-style Italian-American fare, while The Gaslight Club, a restaurant with a Roaring Twenties motif, specializes in seafood and steak and features nightly entertainment.

And, for those with just enough time for a quick sandwich or refreshment, there's the Sports Edition Bar and Grill. Located adjacent to Andiamo, this lively establishment contains all kinds of sports memorabilia, including hundreds of autographed photographs of sports heroes from the past and present.

For guests who prefer to participate in rather than observe athletic activities, the Hilton offers an indoor pool, an aerobic fitness area, weight-lifting facilities, and, as mentioned, the popular simulated golf center.

Despite its close proximity to O'Hare's runways, guests are hard pressed to detect any aircraft noise within the Hilton. That's because all of the public and private rooms are equipped with sound-resistant windows. In addition, the hotel is adjacent to the airport's control tower. That means no jets legally can fly directly over the building.

ABOVE: IDEALLY SITUATED AT THE CROSSROADS OF THE NATION'S AIR ROUTES, THE O'HARE HILTON HOTEL IS A CONVENIENT MEETING PLACE FOR REGIONAL, NATIONAL, AND INTERNATIONAL BUSINESS CONFERENCES.

Chicago Aviation Partners

The creative and management force behind O'Hare's first-class concession program

When organizing design teams for the new International Terminal at Chicago O'Hare International Airport, officials considered only the top consultants in each field. McDonald's Corporation and Duty Free International Inc. (DFI) joined forces in order to optimize their chances of getting involved in the planning process. The organizations pooled their resources, each contributing ideas in its own area of expertise, and created Chicago Aviation Partners (CAP). These efforts paid off, because in 1993, CAP was selected by the City of Chicago to develop, lease, and manage the terminal's entire concession program.

DFI, founded in 1983, is the leading operator of duty-free and retail stores along the United States' Canadian and Mexican borders and in international airports throughout the country. DFI is also the major provider of merchandise for international airlines' in-flight duty-free vendors. All together, DFI serves travelers at 160 duty-free and retail shops throughout the United States, Puerto Rico, the Virgin Islands, Aruba, Saint Martin, Bonaire, and Curacao. DFI has built a world-renowned reputation for understanding the traveling public, offering top-quality brand-name merchandise, convenience, value, and exceptional customer service.

Boasting more than 18,000 locations worldwide, McDonald's Corporation is the world's premier restaurant chain. Travelers recognize and take comfort in the high standards long established and consistently maintained by the "Golden Arches." Moreover, with a portfolio of more than 45 airport restaurants, McDonald's has proven to be the choice of passengers who demand recognizable quality, value, and quick service.

Passengers, visitors, and airport employees alike will enjoy the first-class concession area designed by CAP. The food court features popular eateries such as McDonald's,

Pizzeria Uno, Gold Coast Dogs, Windy City Yogurt, Lou Mitchell's Express, and Parades Bar, all recognized for their Chicago roots. This way, from the moment they arrive until their departure, visitors get a taste of the true Chicago experience.

The terminal's shopping section is a buyer's dream. The 5,500-square-foot Chicago Duty Free store brings the world's premium brands and products to consumers' fingertips. Fenton Hill Florida's upscale news and gift boutiques are ideal for shoppers looking for Chicago-themed merchandise.

As passengers depart the food court, they will come to a large-format four-screen video system, which showcases the breadth of Chicago's magnificent cultural scene with a fascinating video montage. Details such as this make the terminal concession area complete. By focusing on the needs of consumers, Chicago Aviation Partners successfully provides products and services that appeal to travelers, all the while reminding visitors about the pleasures of this world-class city.

BOTH PHOTOS ABOVE: CHICAGO AVIATION PARTNERS, BACKED BY THE EXPERTISE OF ITS PARENT COMPANIES, DESIGNED A SPECTACULAR CONCESSION AREA FOR O'HARE'S INTERNATIONAL TERMINAL.

W H Smith

A world-class literary oasis — and much more — for today's hurried traveler

The bustling newspaper, magazine, and paperback bookstores and bookstalls operated by W H Smith throughout O'Hare's terminals 1, 2 and 3 are magnets for the 200,000-plus people who pass through the airport every day.

W H Smith's stores and stands are essential stops for passengers desiring reading material following or during their flight. Whether travelers want to catch up on the news of the day, read a current best-selling novel, or browse through the latest issue of their favorite magazine, W H Smith stores are bound to have the periodical or book they are seeking.

W H Smith establishments also feature a wide range of unique gift items and souvenirs. T-shirts depicting Chicago's local sports teams or Chicago landmarks are especially popular with visitors passing through O'Hare International.

"We carry Chicago Bulls T-shirts and gear and Chicago Cubs and White Sox T-shirts," says Clive Sills, the chief operating officer of W H Smith's airport division. "We even have a T-shirt extolling Chicago's world-renowned pizza. One of our most popular line of T-shirts depicts Chicago's truly magnificent downtown skyline."

Altogether, W H Smith operates 30 shops and employs some 250 people inside O'Hare International. In addition to 24 newsstands and gift shops, the company recently

added two music stores and four specialty bookstores at the airport.

W H Smith's The Wall music stores — one located on Concourse B in Terminal 1 and the other in Terminal 3 — carry about 4,000 compact disc and audiocassette titles. These stores also carry a large selection of electronic equipment on which the music can be played. W H Smith's specialty bookstores, called Waterstone's Booksellers, carry about 8,000 book titles. Located in Concourse B, Concourse F, Concourse L, and Terminal 3 at O'Hare, these shops provide travelers with a larger selection of reading materials.

"The music shops and specialty bookstores are recent additions," Sills notes. "We put them in because

we didn't feel we were fully satisfying the travel needs of consumers at the airport with just our newsstands."

W H Smith itself is a relatively new addition to O'Hare, having taken over the newsstands at the airport from the previous owner in 1987. Moreover, this Atlanta-based company has only been in existence since 1985. The firm's parent, however, the W H Smith Group plc, based in Great Britain, has been in the newspaper and bookselling business for more than 200 years.

The group's United States division is the largest vendor of newspapers and periodicals in the country, operating approximately 159 newsstands and bookstores in 16 U.S. airports, as well as numerous freestanding The Wall music and Waterstone's Booksellers stores, mostly in the Northeast. Major hotels across the nation, such as Chicago's own Hyatt Regency, also house W H Smith newsstands and bookstores. Overall, the company employs more than 4,000 people nationwide.

BOTH PHOTOS ABOVE: CONVENIENTLY LOCATED THROUGHOUT O'HARE INTERNATIONAL AIRPORT, W H SMITH'S WATERSTONE'S BOOKSELLERS SPECIALTY BOOKSTORES OFFER A WIDE SELECTION OF READING MATERIALS. MORE THAN 8,000 TITLES COVER THE FULL RANGE OF CUSTOMERS' INTERESTS AND NEEDS.

NETWORKS
CHAPTER EIGHT

Ameritech Corp.

At the forefront of the global information and communications transformation

Take a population more than four times the 3 million people who inhabit Chicago. Imagine getting those people, many of whom live hundreds or thousands of miles apart, together — to conduct business, take a college-credit course, share recipes, make a date, or extend birthday or holiday greetings.

Sound far-fetched? Ameritech Corp., one of seven Baby Bells created following the breakup of the Bell system in 1983, does it 200 million times every day through its state-of-the-art telephone, cellular, paging, data, video, and information networks.

Chicago-based Ameritech began in 1984, providing local telephone service in the Great Lakes region, building on the 100-year heritage of its five Midwest Bell companies. But in the little more than a decade that it has been in business, its horizons and the services it provides have expanded far beyond linking 11 million homes and about 1 million businesses via traditional telephone services in Illinois, Indiana, Michi-

gan, Ohio, and Wisconsin. It now does business in all 50 states and in 40 countries, providing a broad range of sophisticated communications services.

Today, Ameritech and its 66,000 employees also provide local and long-distance cellular phone service to 2.3 million individuals and businesses in the Great Lakes region, as well as Missouri, Hawaii, Norway, and Poland; two-way electronic paging to 1 million consumers and businesses in its five-state region, plus Missouri and Minnesota; telephone directories and advertising services for 40 million directory users in the Midwest; and leased communications equipment to some 3,500 businesses and government units across the United States.

Recently, the $13 billion company embarked on a host of interactive video services. As a result, it now provides real-time access to patient records, billing, and clinical transactions for health care providers via net-

works of computer software, hardware, and telephone lines. Through its CivicLink service, available across the U.S. and Canada, Ameritech provides computer software, hardware, and telephone connections to bring government documents such as court and real estate records to the computers of lawyers, real estate agents, or anyone else who has need for such information. And Ameritech is teaming with GE to bring electronic commerce capabilities to businesses around the globe.

By acquiring two security firms — SecurityLink in December 1994 and The National Guardian Corp. in October 1995 — Ameritech currently monitors security alarms for nearly 340,000 homes and businesses in 21 states and Canada. It provides library software for more than 3,700 libraries across the globe, including the Library of Congress. It has invested in the Peapod home grocery-shopping service used by more than 1,000 people in Chicago and San Francisco

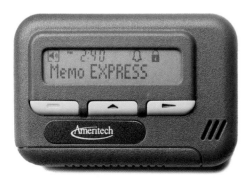

ABOVE AND TOP PHOTO: AMERITECH'S SCOPE RANGES FROM PAGERS AND PAGING SERVICES TO ON-LINE ACCESS.

who shop via their personal computers, modems, and telephone lines. And it connects students, teachers, and educational resources at hundreds of schools, colleges, and universities in the Midwest through interactive video and computer links. In little more than a decade, Ameritech has transformed itself into an all-encompassing communications company.

Ameritech, in fact, is striving to become a one-stop provider of the full range of communications needed by businesses, professionals, educators, and individual consumers — a kind of general store where one can go for all of the latest telephone, wireless, computer, cable, and video technologies needed to help people work, learn, and communicate better in a complex global society.

"Customers say they want the convenience of full service from one company, so we offer a full menu of services — telephone, cellular, paging, data, video, and more," says Richard C. Notebaert, Ameritech's chairman and chief executive officer.

Toward that end, Ameritech is launching into cable television and a host of additional interactive services. Through a joint venture with Walt Disney Company, BellSouth, GTE, and SBC Communications, it is developing, acquiring, packaging, and marketing entertainment, educational, and interactive programming. The venture (named Americast), among other things, is developing services such as video-on-demand and networked video games that can be offered via Ameritech's two-way video network.

Perhaps the company's most ambitious goal, however, is to get into the long-distance telephone business, which would complete the array of communications choices it can offer its customers. Ameritech will be going head to head with AT&T, other long-distance providers, and cable TV companies that are planning to be full-service communications companies, too.

Ameritech took a major step toward becoming a long-distance provider in 1993, filing a bold proposal with the Federal Communications Commission that would open its local telephone network to long-distance providers in exchange for the ability to offer long-distance service to its customers. In return, Ameritech agreed to allow long-distance providers and other communications companies to compete against it in the local telephone market.

Ameritech is not content to be a Midwest, U.S., or even a North American communications company. With information becoming more global, it aims to expand internationally; and, in fact, has already done so.

Ameritech is a major shareowner of Telecom Corporation of New Zealand Limited, that country's principal telecommunications provider. It also has a stake in MATAV, which provides local and long-distance service in Hungary; in Centertel, which supplies cellular service to Poland; in NetCom, Norway's leading digital cellular communications service; and in Belgacom, the national telecommunications provider of Belgium. It also has cellular interests in China and is exploring other communications business opportunities in Europe and the Pacific Rim.

"In a world where anyone can use new communications services to work, shop, bank, and learn, Ameritech will be in the forefront of this transformation," says Notebaert.

BOTH PHOTOS: AMERITECH, WITH ADDITIONAL HOLDINGS IN POLAND (ABOVE), NORWAY, AND BELGIUM, PROVIDES CELLULAR PHONE AND INTERACTIVE VIDEO SERVICES, MAKING IT POSSIBLE TO SEND AND ACCESS CRITICAL INFORMATION (LEFT) AROUND THE WORLD.

Unisys Corporation

Innovative information-based solutions that aid in airlines' survival and growth

Unisys Corporation is one of the largest providers of information services and computer technology and software in the world.

Based in Blue Bell, Pennsylvania, this firm helps 200 airlines worldwide — including 17 of the world's top 25 — with such operations as streamlining passenger reservations, cultivating customer satisfaction, increasing marketing effectiveness, identifying profitable customers, enhancing revenues, and making more timely, effective decisions.

In an era where the business of running an airline is characterized by large costs and thin profit margins, that kind of assistance is exactly what airlines need to survive and prosper.

Unisys offers support systems unique to the airline business. These services include customer management solutions that help transportation organizations deliver superior service, differentiating them from their competitors; air freight management solutions that help airlines and freight forwarders meet the increasing pressure of shippers' demands; and operational solutions that make processing passengers at airports easier, faster, more efficient, and less labor intensive. The company even has a weather information services group that provides airport operators and individual airlines with a range of modern meteorological equipment and data services.

Unisys also creates customized systems to help an airline meet specific needs. When Chicago-based United Airlines wanted to increase revenue and market share generated by freight

forwarders, Unisys developed a software program that enabled the forwarders to obtain real-time flight schedules, check space availability aboard aircraft, and track shipments in transit.

Unisys, however, is not just an airline services firm or even solely a transportation company. Its software, computers, and consulting services are also employed in the fields of financial services, communications, health information management, and government.

In fact, Unisys employees serve 50,000 firms, organizations, and government agencies in 100 countries. Its clients include 41 of the 50 world's largest banks, 31 of the world's largest railways, 35 of the world's largest telecommunications companies, and more than 1,600 governmental bodies worldwide, including the Internal Revenue Service.

Since its inception in 1987, as a result of the merger between computer giants Burroughs Corp. and Sperry Corp., Unisys has been committed to building long-term relationships with its clients, helping them to creatively use information and technology to improve service to their customers and enhance their competitive position in the marketplace.

For more information, contact the Unisys Transportation Home Page at http://www.corp.unisys.com/trans.

TOP PHOTO: MORE THAN 200 AIRLINES AROUND THE WORLD DEPEND ON UNISYS FOR THEIR PASSENGER RESERVATIONS. BOTTOM PHOTO: WHEN LUFTHANSA RECOGNIZED THAT IT NEEDED A SINGLE SYSTEM FOR ITS WORLDWIDE CARGO ACTIVITIES, IT CHOSE UNISYS.

PLANNING & DEVELOPMENT

CHAPTER NINE

PHOTO BY WAYNE CABLE©

Landrum & Brown

A paramount provider of airport facility and operations planning services worldwide

When it comes to providing high-quality professional planning services to the commercial aviation industry, few, if any, consulting firms can beat the track record or expertise of Landrum & Brown.

In 1949, airline veterans Charles Landrum and John Brown established this Cincinnati-based, privately owned aviation planning firm. Since then, most major airport authorities, aviation agencies, and U.S. airlines have turned to Landrum & Brown for assistance in planning airport facilities and operations.

Whether projects involve developing air traffic forecasts, laying the groundwork for a new airport, expanding an existing airfield, building a new terminal or some other airport-

TOP PHOTO: THE CONSULTATION SERVICES OF LANDRUM & BROWN ENSURE O'HARE INTERNATIONAL AIRPORT'S POSITION AS ONE OF THE COUNTRY'S FOREMOST SOURCES OF AIR TRANSPORTATION. ABOVE: THIS STATE-OF-THE-ART CONTROL TOWER IS PART OF O'HARE'S RECENT $2 MILLION EXPANSION PROGRAM.

related facility, or figuring out the best way to finance an airport construction project, Landrum & Brown has the necessary experts, analytical tools, and skills to meet its clients' needs. And, unlike most consulting firms, Landrum & Brown's practice, as well as the work of its more than 125 professionals and support personnel, is almost solely devoted to aviation.

"Our primary business for the last 47 years has been focused on the field of aviation and airport planning," says Jeff Thomas, Landrum & Brown's president. "We believe that our focus on the specialized problems and issues of the aviation industry provides us with a level of expertise that cannot be matched by other organizations whose primary business is not serving the aviation industry."

Landrum & Brown boasts an impressive record of accomplishments. The firm's planning services have been utilized at 21 of the top 25 air-

ports and at 40 of the top 50 airports in the United States, including Chicago O'Hare International and Midway airports. It has also conducted planning studies for several international airports, including those in Berlin and Bonn, Germany; Helsinki, Finland; Toronto and Calgary, Canada; Sydney, Australia; Jeddah, Saudi Arabia; and Belfast, Northern Ireland.

From its major offices located in Chicago, Los Angeles, and Cincinnati, the firm offers four broad areas of aviation advisory services to its clients: facilities and operations planning, terminal planning, environmental planning, and finance and program implementation planning. By combining these services, Landrum & Brown has the unique capability to assist airport authorities and airlines in implementing large-scale projects, from plan conception and design through financing, environmental approval, and management of the new facilities.

"In fact, the only things we don't do in connection with an airport project are to lay the bricks and spread the concrete," says Ken Sura, an official in Landrum & Brown's Chicago office. "We do, however, advise our clients on the correct sequencing of actual construction work."

Project teams are organized for each client assignment. Teams are composed of individuals who have the necessary academic background, training, and experience to successfully and efficiently carry out the assignment. As a result, the firm is able to respond directly, quickly, and economically to clients' needs at each stage of an airport improvement project.

Since its inception, Landrum & Brown has provided airport facilities and operations planning services, applying highly specialized analytical skills to solve problems specifically relating to these areas. Emerging trends in the aviation industry are also addressed in order to meet each client's future needs. The goal is to produce practical, economical, and operationally feasible plans for airport facilities and operations. This service usually includes airport master plans, airfield and airspace capacity plans, and construction and operations plans.

Master plans define the stages of development for airport facilities, accounting for forecast levels of air traffic demand, maximum operational effectiveness, minimum cost, and minimum adverse environmental impact. This calls for a determination of facility requirements and a thorough evaluation of the consequences of all reasonable and practicable options. Such studies culminate in the preparation of detailed airport plans and an economic feasibility analysis.

Airfield and airspace capacity planning is a service that Landrum & Brown has provided since 1972. In fact, the company leads the industry in addressing airspace and airfield problems through the use of simulation modeling and other sophisticated analytic techniques. Use of simulation modeling began with the 1974-1975 O'Hare Airport Delay Task Force Study and continues today in

ABOVE LEFT: LANDRUM & BROWN PLANNED AND IMPLEMENTED UNITED AIRLINES' TERMINAL OF TOMORROW AT O'HARE. BELOW: THIS FIRM'S EXPERT CONSULTATION SERVICES IN TERMINAL DESIGN AND AIRSPACE OPERATIONS HELP KEEP CONGESTION TO A MINIMUM.

conjunction with ongoing airspace performance studies at O'Hare, Midway, and other large international airports around the globe. The firm has conducted similar studies for major airlines, including Continental, United, American, and Qantas.

"While all of these airlines have in-house operations-research groups that could provide similar functions, each retained Landrum & Brown to assist them because of our proven capability to produce meaningful answers to airport capacity questions within short time constraints," says Thomas.

As for airport construction and operations planning, Landrum & Brown

ABOVE: LANDRUM & BROWN'S PLAN-NING SERVICES HAVE BEEN UTILIZED AT 21 OF THE TOP 25 AIRPORTS AND AT 40 OF THE TOP 50 AIRPORTS IN THE UNITED STATES, INCLUDING O'HARE.

is uniquely qualified to help solve the problem of trying to expand, upgrade, or improve airport facilities while still maintaining a safe environment and a high level of service for airport personnel and airline passengers.

Planning for a new airport terminal or for modifications to an existing terminal facility is another area where Landrum & Brown has always been an innovator. Among the services that the firm is capable of providing in this area are conceptual and technical planning and computer simulation and modeling. The firm also has the capability of providing virtually any type of specialized terminal study that a client might require.

Conceptual and technical planning involves taking forecasts of aircraft operations and passenger activity at an airport and translating them into quantifiable amounts of space that will be needed for a new terminal or adding space to an existing facility.

Such a study sets the stage for the actual design and eventual construction of the terminal or addition.

To make accurate forecasts and come up with an appropriate terminal design, Landrum & Brown utilizes a variety of specialized computer programs that it designed. The company's AIRSIM & GATESIM software, for example, is used in conjunction with its terminal planning expertise to determine the most efficient apron and taxiway configurations for an airport. PEOPLEMOVER, another Landrum & Brown computer program, models the level of service to be provided by the major functional areas of a terminal building. Three-dimensional models can be created so that planners and clients can visualize and animate walk-throughs and flybys of proposed terminal facilities.

Specialized studies may include determining optimum revenue-generating opportunities and concession locations within a terminal design and assessing ways to keep proposed terminals adequately maintained.

Environmental planning, especially with respect to noise and air quality, has become an increasingly important part of airport development since the passage of the National Environmental Policy Act of 1969, and Landrum & Brown has been in the forefront of this specialized field since its enactment.

"Our understanding of noise problems, and the associated political implications, and our extensive experience in the field contribute significantly to our ability to assist airport operators in the development of aeronautically implementable noise compatibility plans," Thomas points out.

Landrum & Brown has extensive experience in putting together environmental impact studies, which are required before airport development projects can be implemented. It also has an admirable record when it comes to obtaining environmental approvals from government agencies for airport construction programs. The firm even assists airport operators in coordinating and preparing for public meetings with local citizens to explain airport development proposals and answer questions about the likely environmental impacts of such developments.

"Because of our commitment to public participation through intensive involvement with public officials and affected neighbors, our staff is able to develop credibility for the airport study process and to more clearly understand issues that concern local leaders and residents," says Thomas.

The most critical part of airport development is coming up with the financing necessary to undertake and complete the project. Landrum & Brown's staff has experience in developing project financial studies, including revenue bond financial feasibility studies, marketing studies, business plans, management information systems, and ac-

1961

1946

counting systems. In terms of financial and management services, Landrum & Brown also has the capability of undertaking studies that forecast aviation demand, provide market analysis, and suggest ways to optimize revenues from airport concessions. The firm even assists airport owners and operators in developing and negotiating use agreements with airport tenants, airlines, and concessionaires.

In fact, Landrum & Brown helped plan, implement, and finance O'Hare's recent $2 billion expansion program. In addition, the company acted as the financial feasibility consultant for the more than $1 billion O'Hare General Airport Revenue Bond Issue since 1990. It also prepared and supported O'Hare's tenant special-facility bond issues for Delta, American, and United airlines.

FROM BOTTOM TO TOP, AN AERIAL VIEW OF THE SAME AREA SHOWS THE DEVELOPMENT OF THE WORLD'S BUSIEST AIRPORT, MADE POSSIBLE, IN LARGE PART, BY LANDRUM & BROWN. HISTORIC ORCHARD FIELD (LEFT) EVOLVED INTO THE O'HARE OF THE 1960S (MIDDLE LEFT), WHICH EMERGED AS THE O'HARE OF TODAY (TOP LEFT).

Ricondo & Associates, Inc.

Offering a wide range of aviation planning, environmental, and financial services

Ricondo & Associates, Inc., began in 1989 with less than a handful of employees and a single contract. Since then, the firm has blossomed into one of the nation's premier independent airport planning firms.

Today, Ricondo & Associates boasts a staff of professionals and support personnel located in Cincinnati, Miami, San Antonio, and Alexandria, in addition to its Chicago headquarters. And the firm has earned consulting contracts with airport authorities, airlines, and aircraft manufacturers from Washington, D.C., to California. In addition to airport master planning, Ricondo & Associates also offers airport owners and operators, the airlines, and local, state, and federal aviation agencies a complete line of environmental, financial, and aviation planning services.

Since its inception, Ricondo & Associates has consulted on numerous aviation facilities' planning and environmental impact studies related to O'Hare. Since its founding, the firm has provided a variety of technical support and planning services for Chicago's Department of Aviation, and has also worked on projects involving Chicago's Midway Airport.

RICONDO
& ASSOCIATES

"Working on projects at O'Hare International, the world's busiest airport, gives a firm instant marketing power," says Ramon Ricondo, the company's founder.

Outside Chicago, the firm has served as a planning consultant on projects at Washington's National, Dulles International, San Francisco International, Miami International, and San Antonio International airports, to name a few. The firm has also acted as feasibility consultant and airport consultant for such clients as the Port of Oakland, Reno/Tahoe International, Dayton International, Jackson International, and Charleston International airports. It has been retained by the Federal Aviation Administration to undertake airport environmental impact studies and has also been hired by airlines and aircraft manufacturers to undertake a variety of studies.

When United Airlines, for example, recently became the lead customer for the Boeing Company's new Boeing 777 aircraft, it retained Ricondo & Associates to assess the impact the aircraft would have on a number of airports that United serves around the globe. The study identified facility issues that an airline might face accommodating the 777, the largest twin-engine jet aircraft made to date.

As a result of its rapid growth, Ricondo & Associates today has the ability to deliver a wide range of specialized aviation planning services through distinct practice areas, including airport facilities and operations planning, construction and implementation planning, airport environmental services, and financial planning.

Each practice area is directed by a principal of the firm who has significant experience in his or her area of specialization as well as longtime experience either working at an airport or within the commercial airline industry. In fact, the firm's senior offi-

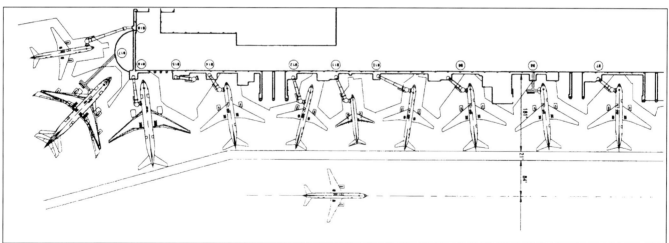

cers have, on average, more than 20 years' experience in the aviation business. All of them have spent years working in aviation consulting, with Ricondo & Associates or with other aviation planning firms. Most also have worked either for one of the airlines, for the Federal Aviation Administration, or with an airport operator.

Ricondo & Associates is distinguished from other airport consulting firms in that its sole focus is on aviation planning. The company commits itself to supporting its clients from the very beginning of the planning and design process all the way to the end of the construction and/or implementation phase.

"We are guided by a philosophy that makes clients' needs and service delivery our top priorities," Ricondo says. "It's that kind of commitment and performance that has built long-term relationships for our firm."

UBM, Inc.

Constructing Chicago's present and future — its airports, schools, hospitals, bridges

Constructing a brand-new International Terminal at O'Hare International Airport, rehabilitating Chicago's Soldier Field, and building a dormitory for naval recruits at the Great Lakes Naval Training Center north of Chicago are vastly different types of development projects. UBM, Inc., however, has participated as a major player in all of them.

In fact, this 22-year-old firm, the largest African American owned and operated construction services company in Illinois, has been a part of every major public works project and several private development projects in the Windy City since its inception.

Currently, with a staff of more than 60 construction and engineering specialists, it continues to provide general contracting, construction management, and program management, as well as specialty contracting services, to a broad, diverse range of clients. Included in this client list are the Chicago public school and library systems; Chicago Transit Authority; Northern Trust Bank; Northwestern Memorial and Mount Sinai hospitals; and such religious institutions as the Trinity United Church of Christ.

THE TAESA AIRLINES TERMINAL (PICTURED ABOVE) AND THE NEW INTERNATIONAL TERMINAL (AT RIGHT), BOTH LOCATED AT CHICAGO O'HARE INTERNATIONAL AIRPORT, ARE TWO OF THE MANY CONSTRUCTION ACCOMPLISHMENTS OF UBM, INC.

Founded by construction industry veterans Paul King, Sandra Jiles, and Sham Dabadghao, and incorporated in 1975, UBM bases its success on the fact that it brings the following philosophy to each project: Provide each client, no matter how big or small, with the highest standard of quality service and materials, consistent on-time performance, and a job completed under budget.

"We established this philosophy with our very first project in the mid-1970s, a $46 million joint-venture development of a new University of Illinois hospital in Chicago," says Sham Dabadghao, UBM's chief technical officer. "We garnered some important credentials with that first development. In fact, we were Illinois' first minority firm to offer construction management services for such a project. And more importantly, by completing the work ahead of schedule, we saved the University of Illinois close to $1 million."

The firm also believes in working harmoniously with its clients and its development partners in order to

achieve the successful completion of projects. Over its two decades, UBM has participated as a joint-venture partner with major Chicago and national construction firms on such large public works projects as the $650 million, 1.2-million-square-foot state-of-the-art O'Hare International Terminal; the $750 million expansion of the McCormick Place Convention Center in Chicago; the recent $250 million Chicago public schools construction and renovation program; the

$26 million renovation of the Cook County Juvenile Court and Detention Center; and the $20 million renovation of Soldier Field, Chicago's lakefront sports palace that is home to professional football's Chicago Bears.

The firm also has participated as a general contractor in such key capital improvements as the $6.5 million restoration of the historic Reliance Building in downtown Chicago, the $2.5 million rehabilitation of the Chicago Skyway Bridge, and the $16.2 million construction of a student residence hall and union at Chicago State University.

In Chicago's private sector, it has taken part in the construction of a 310,000-square-foot airport facility for Federal Express Corp., a $2.4 million waste-processing facility for Waste Management of North America, and the $1.3 million renovation of the Brickyard Mall Shopping Center.

Moreover, UBM continues to play a role in the ongoing upgrading of Chicago's airport system. Just recently, it took part in the renovation

work undertaken by the city's Department of Aviation in the terminal at Midway Airport.

UBM offers a wide range of building and infrastructure construction services. Its general contracting division provides general construction contracting, in-house expertise in concrete pouring, carpentry, and hoisting package services.

A second division, the construction and program management unit, provides construction management and consulting services, estimating and construction scheduling services, construction feasibility services, project and contract administration, architectural-related services, construction inspection services, and value engineering.

UBM, however, brings much more than its long-time experience and its staff of professional architects, construction managers, and civil, structural, mechanical, and environmental engineers to a development project.

"Unlike many firms, we bring significant bonding capabilities that are critical to successfully undertaking

and completing large-scale construction jobs," notes Sandra Jiles, UBM's president.

For example, when Turner Construction Co., a major building firm, recently needed a partner who could meet its rigorous bonding, scheduling, and technical capability requirements to build the foundation for an $83 million, 525,000-square-foot health care facility for the University of Chicago Hospitals, it had no qualms about turning to UBM.

Paul King, UBM's chairman and a long-time advocate for increased minority participation in the construction industry, says, "It's taken 20 years of hard work to bring our firm to the respected position we've achieved in the construction and public works field. Now our goal is to continue to grow and take on ever-larger and more challenging assignments."

ABOVE: UBM'S VISIONARY PRINCIPALS, PHOTOGRAPHED FROM LEFT TO RIGHT, ARE PAUL KING, SHAM DABADGHAO, AND SANDRA JILES.

K-Five Construction Corp.

Laying the foundation for O'Hare International and Chicago — past, present, future

With three generations of construction experience to draw upon, K-Five Construction Corp. has in just two decades of existence grown into one of largest and most respected road building and pavement resurfacing companies in the Chicago area.

This Lemont-based firm was established in 1977, but its history really dates back to nearly the turn of the century. That's when the current owners' maternal grandfather, William J. Newman, operated a well-known Chicago construction firm that did much of the caisson work

ABOVE AND RIGHT: DEDICATED PROFESSIONALS AND STATE-OF-THE-ART EQUIPMENT HAVE MADE IT POSSIBLE FOR K-FIVE TO BECOME ONE OF THE STATE'S LARGEST ROAD BUILDING AND PAVEMENT RESURFACING COMPANIES.

upon which many of the city's skyscrapers currently stand.

In addition, the owners' paternal grandfather, George Krug, also was well-known in the construction business in the first half of the twentieth century. Krug operated an excavating firm that, among other things, dug the foundations for many of the historic buildings in downtown Chicago.

William J. Newman and George Krug were respected as two of Chicago's preeminent leaders in the construction field.

"In effect, K-Five is the product of the merger through marriage of the Newman and Krug families," says Jody Krug, one of the five grandchildren who hold an interest in the company.

Currently, three of the five grandchildren play an active role in the firm. George Krug, Jr., who started working for Krug Excavating Co. more than 30 years ago, serves as K-Five's president and guiding

force, personally reviewing and setting the final price on 95 percent of the 1,200-plus construction cost estimates the firm produces every year and signing a majority of the company's contracts. Rob Krug is active in field management, equipment purchasing, and union negotiations. Jody Krug is involved in administration and marketing.

To their credit, K-Five has steadily grown from a company with sales of $680,000 into a corporation with annual revenues in excess of $100 million, making it one of the largest road construction companies in Illinois. More importantly, the company has been profitable each year it has been in existence.

In addition to its Lemont headquarters, K-Five has facilities at many other Chicago-area locations where it stores and maintains its vast fleet of equipment, operates four portable concrete plants, and runs five asphalt manufacturing facilities.

What makes K-Five successful, according to Rob Krug, are the dedicated people who work for the

company (the firm employs 500 to 550 people during the construction season) and its principles of honesty and versatility. Moreover, no pavement construction job is too big, too small, or too complicated for K-Five to handle. All clients, be they large government agencies, privately owned businesses, or private individuals, are given the same attention and professional level of service.

K-Five has been the successful low bidder for contracts on the construction and reconstruction of many of the tollways, expressways, and major highways in Northern Illinois, including the reconstruction of the Kennedy Expressway a couple of years ago, the construction of the Interstate 355 toll road, and the recent reconstruction of the Tri-State Tollway (I-294).

The company has also succeeded in winning several hundred million dollars worth of contracts from the City of Chicago and other government agencies operating within the metropolitan area. Not long ago, K-Five completed pavement construction work for the city's Department of Aviation at the new International Terminal at O'Hare International Airport. In addition, the firm has done taxiway, holding apron, and runway resurfacing work at O'Hare International and at Chicago's Midway Airport for the aviation department.

In Chicago's suburban area, the company has completed a variety of resurfacing contracts for dozens of municipalities extending from the far-north suburban areas to Northwest Indiana.

In the private sector, K-Five has completed pavement work at O'Hare International for United Airlines' new terminal, and the firm has constructed, expanded, or refurbished taxiways and tarmacs at O'Hare for such airlines as Delta, Northwest, Lufthansa, Air France, Flying Tiger, and Federal Express. Maintaining an expertise in transportation, K-Five has paved intermodal facilities for numerous railroads, including Union Pacific, Chicago and Northwestern, and Illinois Central.

Also in the private sector, K-Five paved the parking lots at Chicago's McCormick Place convention and exhibition center; at the new Comiskey Park, home of major-league baseball's White Sox; and at the newly constructed United Center, home of pro basketball's Chicago Bulls team and hockey's Chicago Black Hawks team.

BOTH PHOTOS ABOVE: K-FIVE'S REPUTATION FOR HIGH-QUALITY WORK RECOMMENDS THE COMPANY TO A GREAT RANGE OF CLIENTS, INCLUDING CHICAGO O'HARE INTERNATIONAL AIRPORT.

HNTB Corporation

More than 50 years' experience in planning and designing airports and other facilities

When it comes to airport planning and development in the United States, chances are good that the HNTB Corporation will be right in the middle of the action.

HNTB, an architectural, engineering, and planning firm, is one of the nation's leading planners and designers of airport facilities. In fact, since the company began providing aviation facility planning, design, and engineering services more than 50 years ago, it has been involved in nearly 1,000 airport projects.

"We estimate that one of every three people who flies in the United States each day flies into or out of an airport where HNTB has worked," says Gerald H. Styler, an HNTB vice president and head of the company's Chicago office.

This Kansas City-based firm designs everything from runways and terminals to the highways and bridges leading into and out of airports. And its staff of engineers and architects has planned or designed just about every type of airfield project imaginable, from military air bases to commercial jetports as large as Chicago O'Hare International Airport.

The Chicago office is one of about three dozen design and field offices that HNTB maintains across the country. Besides airports, the 2,000-employee-strong firm designs a variety of other facilities essential to modern community living, including wastewater-treatment facilities, highways, bridges, schools, industrial parks, office complexes, shopping malls, recreational centers, and convention halls.

In Chicago, where HNTB opened its local office approximately 30 years ago, the firm has played a pivotal role in the ongoing development of O'Hare International and in the expansion and upgrading of Midway Airport, Chicago's first and still-active airfield.

In just the past three years, HNTB's Chicago engineers, along with staff from some of the other HNTB offices, have been involved in more than $180 million worth of local airport improvement projects. And the firm was recently selected to be part of a consortium that will design and oversee the construction of a new passenger terminal at Midway Airport.

O'Hare International, however, is where the firm's talents have really shined, helping to keep the 75-year-old airfield, the world's busiest, from becoming obsolete.

Most recently, HNTB has been involved in designing and coordinating O'Hare's runway resurfacing work, taxiway rehabilitation and expansion, and the construction of new aircraft holding aprons. These projects, undertaken at a cost of more than $35 million, are helping O'Hare reduce delays during peak operating periods.

ABOVE: TAXIWAY G1 AT CHICAGO O'HARE INTERNATIONAL AIRPORT IS SHOWN IN THE FOREGROUND, WITH THE SCENIC HOLD APRON VISIBLE IN THE BACKGROUND.

Airport Owners Representatives

Developing and maintaining the international standing of Chicago's airports

When the City of Chicago needed a team of specialists to oversee the final stages of construction of the new $610 million International Terminal at O'Hare International Airport in 1993, it turned to two Chicago-area development veterans.

Patrick Harbour, president of Harbour Contractors Inc., and Raymond Chin, president of R.M. Chin & Associates, a Chicago-based real estate development and construction management firm, joined forces to create Airport Owners Representatives (AOR). The businessmen's combined expertise more than qualified AOR to supervise the project.

Their joint-venture consulting firm completed the terminal project on time and within budget. As a result, AOR has been overseeing improvements at O'Hare International and Midway airports on behalf of the city's Department of Aviation ever since.

Originally, AOR was to be simply an extension of Harbour Contractors and R.M. Chin; a part-time job for the principals of the two firms. The work, however, proved much more intensive than that.

"AOR has almost become a full-time job for us," says Harbour, whose own construction firm has worked on some of the largest commercial, industrial, transportation, and infrastructure development projects in the Chicago area over the last three decades.

AOR AIRPORT OWNERS REPRESENTATIVES

Supervising Consultant for the City of Chicago Department of Aviation

Indeed, AOR has an enormous assignment; it oversees virtually all of the design work, construction, and financing for the improvements of the city's airports. The full-time staff of more than 65 people works with architects, engineers, consultants, and planners to put together a development plan; oversees the work of subconsultants and subcontractors to ensure that a project is implemented according to plan; and tracks and accounts for every dollar spent.

"We're not only responsible for overseeing major projects such as the renovation or construction of a terminal, but also the day-to-day improvements such as replacing bro-

ken or worn-out terrazzo tiles in the terminals," comments Stephen L. Kozerowitz, a civil engineer and construction technology expert and AOR's managing director.

In 1996 alone, AOR tracked some $153 million worth of improvements, both large and small, at O'Hare and some $80 million at Midway Airport.

Recent AOR projects at O'Hare include the $60 million rehabilitation of the airport's huge enclosed parking garage and the residential sound insulation program. The latter project, implemented jointly by the city and the Federal Aviation Administration, involved soundproofing some 3,500 homes adjacent to the airport, a task that totaled nearly $90 million.

Based on its experience overseeing improvements at Chicago's airports, AOR plans to eventually make its services available to other airport authorities around the nation. For now, they've got "more than enough to handle right here in Chicago," says Kozerowitz.

PHOTOS: AOR IS A KEY PART OF O'HARE AIRPORT'S DEVELOPMENT AND UPKEEP. THE COMPANY SUPERVISED THE CONSTRUCTION OF THE NEW INTERNATIONAL TERMINAL (TOP), AND MANAGES THE OPERATION AND MAINTENANCE OF THE CITY OF CHICAGO'S AUTOMATED TRANSPORTATION SYSTEM (BOTTOM).

Rust Environment & Infrastructure Inc.

Comprehensive engineering to construction management services for nearly 100 years

With a staff of more than 2,800 engineers, engineering technicians, architects, scientists, construction managers, and other professionals, Rust Environment & Infrastructure Inc. takes on daily challenges of herculean proportions.

Expertly solving the complexities of planning new airports; originating environmental impact statements; identifying the most feasible right-of-way for a new rapid transit system, an airport runway, or an interstate highway; and finding an efficient and realistic way to link up an industrial park to a public transportation system are simply par for the course for this formidable organization.

In the area of transportation alone, this environmental consulting firm has done master-planning work, construction management, and environmental studies in connection with the recent renovation of O'Hare International. It has also completed design work for airports in New Orleans, Indianapolis, and Phoenix, and is currently overseeing the construction of Midway Airport's new passenger terminal.

Rust Environment & Infrastructure's expertise, however, is not limited to design work, the planning of transportation facilities, or the management of construction projects. Among the comprehensive services this company offers are regulatory compliance management; environmental services, such as solid-waste management, hazardous-waste management, air-quality control, and wastewater management; and such specialty services as quality assurance and control, construction documentation, and the organizing of programs that involve the community in maintaining a safe environment.

"We offer a full range of investigative, planning, engineering, design, and construction management services to fulfill the individual needs of our customers, which include federal, state, and local government agencies, as well as industrial and commercial organizations," says Dave Williams, vice president of Rust Environment & Infrastructure's Chicago office.

The firm retains a large team of specialists, including experts in computer and geographic information systems, community relations, health and safety, economic development, and industrial hygiene. The organization also has access to the resources of its parent company, WMX Technologies Inc. (formerly known as Waste Management Inc.), the world's largest waste-management establishment.

Rust Environment & Infrastructure's roots date back to 1910, meaning the firm now has nearly a century of experience in environmental and infrastructure consulting for organizations nationwide. Today, it operates out of more than 70 offices across the United States and Mexico.

Poised for the new millennium, Rust Environment & Infrastructure Inc. will continue its commitment to bringing integrity and creativity to each of its assignments — large or small, simple or complex — thus ensuring its continued success.

ABOVE: RUST ENVIRONMENT & INFRA-STRUCTURE INC. PLAYED AN IMPORTANT ROLE IN THE RECENT RENOVATION OF O'HARE AIRPORT. LEFT: GUIDANCE SIGNS ON TAXIWAYS DIRECT TRAFFIC AS DETERMINED BY THE FIRM.

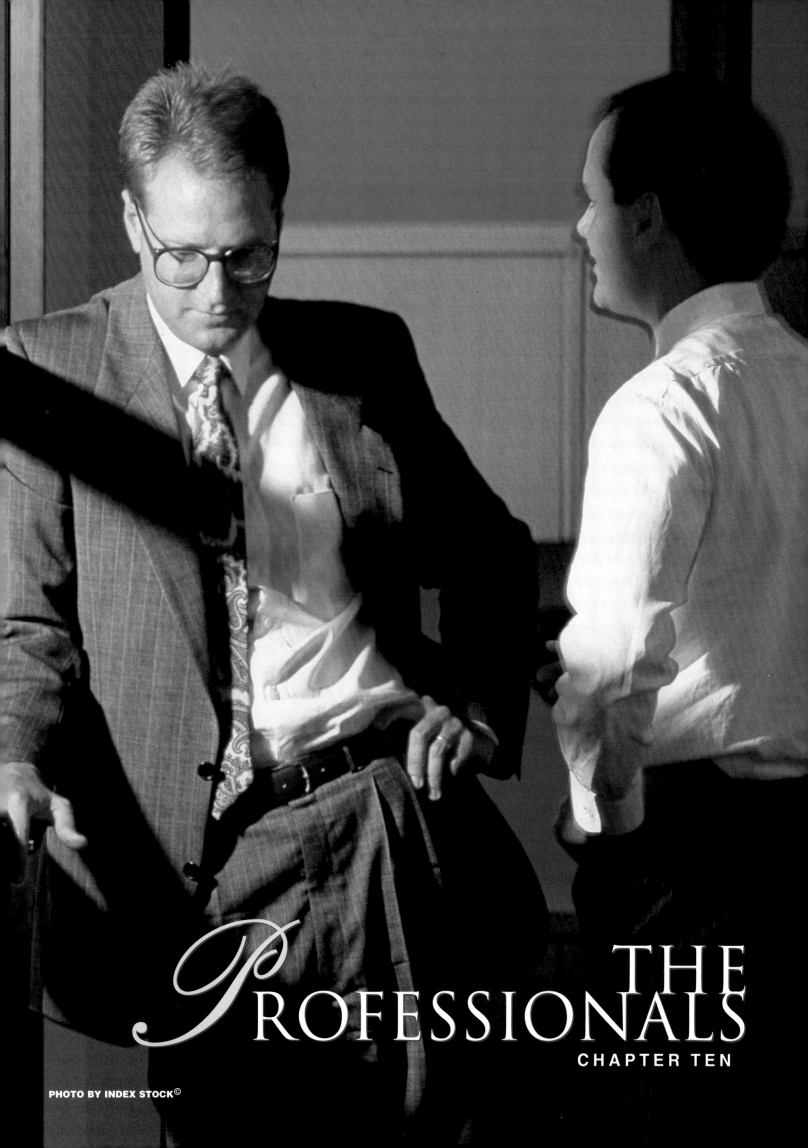

THE PROFESSIONALS

CHAPTER TEN

Allstate Insurance Company

A long-standing commitment to customers and community ... always in "good hands"

That famous slogan — "You're in Good Hands With Allstate" — has been Allstate Insurance Company's trademark for as long as most people can remember. Indeed, it has helped make this insurance firm, based in Northbrook, Illinois, the most recognized brand name in the property-casualty business.

More importantly, however, this motto has long underscored Allstate's commitment to customer service. Based on the number of people who have their automobile and/or homeowners insurance policies with Allstate, it's obvious that the American consumer has taken the "you're in good hands" slogan to heart.

Altogether, Allstate has nearly 30 million auto and homeowners poli-

TOP PHOTO: ALLSTATE'S FAMILY IN-CLUDES ABOUT 15,000 EMPLOYEE-AGENTS AND SOME 2,100 INDEPENDENT AGENTS ACROSS THE U.S. AND CANADA. ABOVE RIGHT: ONE OUT OF EVERY EIGHT CAR AND HOME OWNER IN AMERICA TURNS TO ALLSTATE FOR HIS OR HER INSURANCE POLICY NEEDS.

cies in its portfolio today, making it the nation's largest publicly held personal lines insurer with a healthy 13 percent market share. Also, with about 15,000 full-time employee-agents and some 2,100 independent agents across the United States and Canada, new policies are being added to Allstate's inventory every day.

Allstate attributes its success to knowing what its customers need and want when it comes to insurance. "In business, success comes from knowing your customer," says Jerry D. Choate, chairman and chief executive of The Allstate Corporation, the parent of Allstate Insurance. "In the insurance business, it comes from serving a variety of customers with products that meet their needs and prices that reflect the risk we assume. With more than 65 years of experience and more than 20 million customers, we've learned how to do that very well."

A good deal of Allstate's success also can be attributed to its long-standing commitment to voluntary community service. Through its corporate and local programs, Allstate supports more than 1,400 organizations devoted to improving the quality of life in America. "I see our commit-

ment to community service not only as our responsibility, but also as a requirement for the success of our business," says Choate.

Although Allstate's auto and homeowners insurance polices account for nearly 70 percent of its premiums, the company also sells life insurance, as well as policies covering motorcycles, motor homes, recreational vehicles, boats, apartments, condominiums, and other products. It also markets commercial vehicle and property insurance to small businesses and offers a broad line of personal life insurance, annuity, and group pension products.

In fact, the Allstate Life Insurance Company is the 13th-largest life insurer in the U.S. in terms of life insurance in force, and the 18th-largest based on assets. Although Allstate didn't sell its first life insurance policy until 1957, its life insurance policies today generate more than one-fifth of the corporation's premiums annually and about 15 percent of its operating income. Life insurance is one of the fastest-growing parts of Allstate's business.

Another rapidly growing product is Allstate's nonstandard auto insurance, which covers drivers with poor driving records or those who own "high-performance" automobiles. Through Allstate Indemnity Company, the insurer has more than 2 million such policies in force, making it the country's largest nonstandard auto insurer.

Not a bad track record for a company that got its start 30 years into the twentieth century as a sideline business of a retailing giant, the Chicago-based Sears, Roebuck and Company.

Allstate got its start when, during a friendly game of bridge aboard a Chicago commuter train in 1930, insurance broker Carl Odell suggested to his friend Gen. Robert E. Wood, the chairman of Sears at the time, that Sears could make money selling auto insurance the same way it sold much of its clothing and .appliances … through its celebrated mail-order catalog. Being the visionary businessman that he was, Wood jumped on the suggestion and on April 17, 1931, set up Allstate Insurance as a unit of the "big store" and put Odell in charge. Wood borrowed the Allstate name from an automobile tire sold in the catalog.

Before too long, Allstate was selling automobile insurance out of just about every Sears store in the country, in addition to selling through the catalog. And as Sears grew, so did Allstate, especially after World War II, when suburban housing developments sprang up ever farther from central cities. Owning an automobile became a necessity for residents of the distant new subdivisions; prudence dictated that those automobiles, as well as the new homes, needed to be insured.

Allstate remained a part of Sears (and an increasingly major contributor to its net income) until June 1995,

when Sears, deciding to concentrate on its core retailing business, spun off its remaining stake in the insurer to shareholders of Sears' common stock. Allstate had gone public two years earlier when Sears sold off 19 percent of the insurer's stock to the public for $2.4 billion. It was the largest initial public offering in U.S. history.

Having emerged from Sears' shadow, Allstate began to spread its wings as never before. "Being independent allows us to be more flexible, which is critical in today's fast-paced business environment," Choate says. "It helps us pick up the pace of growth and change. In short, it's a natural evolution that benefits our customers, our employees, and our shareholders."

ABOVE: ALLSTATE IS ONE OF THE MOST RECOGNIZED AND TRUSTED NAMES IN THE PROPERTY-CASUALTY BUSINESS. LEFT: ALLSTATE ALSO TOUCHES COUNTLESS PEOPLE BY DONATING FUNDS AND VOLUNTEERING TIME TO COMMUNITY ORGANIZATIONS. THESE EFFORTS, IN ADDITION TO THE ALLSTATE FOUNDATION (WHICH AWARDS GRANTS TO NONPROFIT ORGANIZATIONS), ARE JUST THE TIP OF ALLSTATE'S COMMUNITY FOCUS.

Aon Risk Services

Insurance and risk management experts, placing clients' goals "first, last, always"

Workers' compensation, environmental risks, professional and product liability, employee benefits — the list of concerns facing business owners and managers today, in addition to making a profit, seems boundless.

To effectively and efficiently contend with such important matters, businesspeople need an experienced, professional insurance broker and risk management consultant. When it comes to experience and professionalism in both areas, few firms can match Aon Risk Services. This retail brokerage and risk management arm of the Chicago-based Aon Corporation is one of the largest insurance brokerage and consulting operations in the world.

Aon Risk Services' professionals are expert in the insurance needs of a wide range of industries, including chemicals, heavy manufacturing, and retail. Moreover, the firm is especially adept at handling the insurance and risk management concerns of companies, large and small, in such highly specialized and complex areas as marine shipping, aviation, construction, health care, technology, hospitality, gaming, and entertainment.

For example, Aon Aviation has more than 100 employees exclusively dedicated to managing the risks of firms with aviation exposures. These experts are acutely

aware of the insurance needs of the wide variety of businesses that compose and service the aviation and space industry.

Like Aon's other industry service groups, Aon Aviation can meet the insurance needs of clients no matter where their operations are located. That's because the unit, like all the others in Aon Risk Services, operates through a network of regional offices. The Aviation team has offices in Chicago, Los Angeles, New York, and Washington, D.C. International client placements and services are coordinated through Nicholson Leslie Aviation, an Aon-owned company based in London.

Continuing communication between the regional offices brings together the talents of Aon Aviation

professionals across the globe. As a result, Aon Aviation has the capability of using the parent firm's entire network as a resource to assist in the production, marketing, and servicing of all aspects of aviation insurance for each and every one of its clients. Among these clients are major and regional airlines, airports, aviation manufacturers, and aircraft lessors.

Through its extensive network of regional offices, Aon Aviation, like other units in Aon Risk Services, can also offer each client a team of consultants to design creative and cost-effective solutions that reduce their exposure to safety risks. Aon safety specialists can, for example, provide expertise in the areas of safety management, ergonomics, training, undertaking physical hazard and employee safety surveys, and OSHA regulations.

What really separates Aon from its competitors in the insurance and risk management field, however, is that each client is treated as if he or she were Aon's sole customer. Each Aon professional cares about each client's business goals "first, last, and always," according to the company's motto.

ABOVE: AON'S WORLD HEADQUARTERS IN CHICAGO OVERSEES ONE OF THE WORLD'S LARGEST INSURANCE BROKERAGE AND CONSULTING OPERATIONS.

Ogilvy Adams & Rinehart

Expert public relations services by the top communications specialists in the field

T he skilled, high-energy public relations counselors at the Chicago office of Ogilvy Adams & Rinehart are among the best in their business. Because of such experts and its medium size, this firm is able to offer its clients all the benefits of a large corporation with the advantage of focused personalized service.

"Two-thirds of our professionals have a minimum of eight years of agency and/or corporate public relations experience," says Marilou von Ferstel, the executive vice president and general manager of Ogilvy Adams & Rinehart's Chicago office. "In addition, many of our people have extensive backgrounds in government or public affairs."

The staff's broad knowledge and varied areas of expertise allow the agency to offer its corporate and institutional clients a wide range of communications services, including seminars on dealing effectively and positively with the news media; establishing good relations with governmental agencies and community groups; and projecting a positive image among investors, employees, customers, and the entire community.

"To remain competitive, businesses must become more global in scope and fundamentally restructure their operations. Communications specialists are essential for this kind of development," says von Ferstel.

ABOVE RIGHT: AS THIS PAINTING ILLUSTRATES, OGILVY ADAMS & RINEHART HELPS ITS CLIENTS TO THINK A FEW STEPS AHEAD.

"And the Chicago office of Ogilvy Adams & Rinehart is uniquely qualified to meet these needs."

Because Ogilvy Adams & Rinehart has branches worldwide, its Chicago office has access to an international communications network. The firm is able to connect its clients with various companies around the world — operations whose employees and managers may differ in terms of culture and in how they define quality — thus ensuring clients that proper region-al marketing tactics will be used and potential consumers will be able to identify with the company's products or services.

Attesting to the success of Ogilvy Adams & Rinehart's Chicago office is its impressive list of Chicago-based nationally known clients, including the Quaker Oats Company; the NutraSweet Company; Navistar International; Helene Curtis; Good Humor-Breyers; the City of Chicago Department of Aviation; and the Art Institute of Chicago.

Hopkins & Sutter

Innovative legal and financial consulting services for O'Hare and other airports

Fifteen years ago, the City of Chicago hired Hopkins & Sutter, a 150-lawyer Chicago-based firm, to assist in the redevelopment of O'Hare International Airport. The assignment: create a financing structure for the $800 million redevelopment program and negotiate a new agreement with the airlines supporting the program.

This 75-year-old law firm did just that, obtaining airline approvals for the issuance of O'Hare's first new airport revenue bonds in 1983. As a result of that experience, Hopkins & Sutter created the first full-fledged airport legal practice in the country.

Since the initial O'Hare project, the Airport Services Group at Hopkins & Sutter has provided innovative counsel in such areas as airline agreements, airport financing, noise and other environmental problems, litigation, government regulations, and airline bankruptcies at nearly 50 airports nationwide. In the process, it has worked on more than 100 airport financings — including programs at 18 of the nation's 25 busiest airports — helping to raise more than $13 billion for airport capital development within the United States.

Having been the first major law firm to establish a legal services unit focused exclusively on airports, Hopkins & Sutter is the most experienced law firm available to help airports implement development plans. And with 10 attorneys assigned to the group, including legislative and regulatory experts based in Hopkins & Sutter's Washington, D.C., office,

no firm has a larger or more diverse contingent of experts devoted to working with airport operators.

"Planning and financing the growth of airports to meet future needs requires a team of professionals with skills and experience," says Lynn Goldschmidt, who has been a member of Hopkins & Sutter's Airport Services Group since its inception in 1981 and who currently serves as the group's chairman. "Hopkins & Sutter's experience in the legal and financial affairs of airports has made us a valuable member of many airport development teams."

Indeed, the law firm's valued counsel and top-notch performance in airport development programs has played and continues to play a key role in the growth of its airport practice. Nearly every airport program the firm takes part in results in referrals that bring in new clients.

The Airport Services Group's list of clients is impressive. In addition

to continuing to provide legal and financial consulting services for O'Hare, the group has been involved in development programs at Washington Dulles International and Washington National airports, New York's LaGuardia and John F. Kennedy International airports, Pittsburgh International Airport, and the new Denver International Airport, to name a few.

Among its most interesting projects, the group came up with a financing structure that enabled the City of Chicago to pay for the construction of O'Hare's new International Terminal based solely on credits of a consortium of international airlines.

ABOVE: HOPKINS & SUTTER'S AIRPORT SERVICES GROUP HAS BEEN AN IMPORTANT PART OF THE TEAM FOR MANY OF O'HARE INTERNATIONAL'S MAJOR UPGRADES AND IMPROVEMENTS.

VISITORS & CONVENTIONS

CHAPTER ELEVEN

Best Western Midway Hotel

Ideally situated and comfortably priced, with thoughtful amenities and service

Business or leisure travelers arriving at Chicago O'Hare International Airport don't have to go far for comfortable accommodations and a warm welcome. The Best Western Midway Hotel, at the intersection of Oakton Street and Busse Road in Elk Grove Village, is just six miles (a 20-minute ride in the hotel's courtesy van) from the airport.

AN INVITING ATRIUM RECREATION AREA (ABOVE) AND A LARGE SYMPOSIUM AUDIOVISUAL THEATER (RIGHT) ARE JUST THE BEGINNING OF THE MIDWAY HOTEL'S MANY AMENITIES.

With 165 guest rooms on three floors, an attentive staff, a casual restaurant and lounge, and a large swimming pool and sauna in an under-glass tropical setting, the Midway is as cozy as a country inn and as relaxing as a cabana on a sun-kissed beach.

Thousands of travelers who come to the Chicago area on business find their way to the Midway. And once they try the hotel's accommodations, relax alongside its picturesque pool, and experience the down-to-earth friendliness of its staff, they usually return again and again.

Robert Morelli, the hotel's general manager thinks he knows why. "It's the comfort factor," he says. "Our hotel has the feel of a home away from home, and so our guests don't feel overwhelmed or intimidated as they might be at some of the larger hotels that dot the landscape around

O'Hare. At the Midway, everything the hotel has to offer is in easy reach and guests and staff members often are on a first-name basis."

Indeed, more than a few business travelers bring their spouses and children to the hotel on some of their business trips and stay the weekend for a family getaway.

"While we cater primarily to business travelers, the fact that we have a heated swimming pool, whirlpool, sauna, and game area enclosed in a huge, spectacular glass atrium, makes our hotel a great place for families to escape for a couple of days," Morelli says. "This tropiclike setting is especially a welcome change of pace in the middle of winter."

The Midway's location near major business centers, shopping malls, and entertainment complexes in Chicago's northwest suburban area also makes it an ideal home away from home. Elk Grove Village's Centex Industrial Park, the nation's largest industrial park, is adjacent to the hotel. The Rosemont Horizon, a stadium that is home to college basketball games, professional indoor soccer and hockey teams, concerts, ice shows and circuses, is just three miles away.

Also nearby is the Woodfield Shopping Mall, the largest indoor shopping facility in the Chicago area. Arlington Park Race Track, the O'Hare Exposition and Convention Center, and a Six Flags Great America theme park are also close. And downtown Chicago is just 20 miles to the southeast.

For groups of 20 or more, the Midway can arrange for charter buses to transport hotel guests to area attractions and business centers. A courtesy van providing transportation to and from the hotel and O'Hare is available.

Increasingly today, for both business and leisure travelers, cost — in addition to amenities and location — is an area of concern. The Midway is ideal on all counts. In addition to its 165 spacious guest rooms featuring double- and king-size beds, the hotel boasts more than a dozen executive-class rooms and four luxurious suites, all reasonably priced.

The Midway, which is affiliated with the Best Western hotel chain but is independently owned, thoughtfully attends to the needs of business travelers. The hotel keeps a coffee maker with coffee in all guest rooms. Executive-class rooms feature personal amenities packages, hair dryers, and shoe buffers. Guests staying in executive-class rooms also receive complimentary luxuries such as a newspaper delivered to their room each morning and a cooked-to-order breakfast and evening hors d'oeuvres served at Jericho's Lounge. The lounge also offers six satellite TVs; a DJ plays dance music nightly.

For those who need to transmit data to the home office before retiring, data port phones are available in each guest room for modem use. Fax service is available at the hotel's front desk.

The Midway also has facilities for business meetings and banquets for up to 250 people. In addition to 13 conference rooms, there's a 100-seat theater with audiovisual capabilities for more formal business presentations or training seminars. Even the pool area can be reserved for business-related cocktail parties and lunches or dinners. It's a setting that even the glitziest high-priced hotels in the O'Hare area can't match.

SPACIOUS GUEST ROOMS (ABOVE) AND FULLY EQUIPPED CONFERENCE SUITES (LEFT) ARE PERFECT FOR THE MIDWAY HOTEL'S VACATIONING AND BUSINESS GUESTS ... AND THEIR FAMILIES.

Carlson Wagonlit Travel

Worldwide, 4,100 offices handle the needs of business, government, leisure travelers

Picture this: You are in Chicago, one colleague is in Moscow, another is in London, and it's up to you to arrange a conference call between yourself and your business associates. With three dramatically different time zones, when is the best hour for the call?

This is an example of the offbeat problems Carlson Wagonlit Travel is prepared to solve for traveling businesspeople. Any agency can book flights, hotel rooms, and rental cars — Carlson Wagonlit believes in going the extra mile on behalf of its clients.

Formed in 1994 through the union of the Minneapolis-based Carlson Travel Network and the Paris-based Wagonlit Travel, Carlson Wagonlit Travel today is one of the two largest travel agencies in the world. In North America alone, the company has more than 1,000 franchised travel agency offices in addition to its company-owned operations. Worldwide, Carlson Wagonlit Travel has a $13.3 billion network of 4,100 offices in 125 countries, and it handles the business travel needs of more than 50,000 major commercial and government clients as well as millions of leisure travelers.

Although Carlson Wagonlit Travel is only a couple of years old, the two firms that were joined together to form the new agency have long and distinguished histories in the travel business.

Carlson Travel Network, a unit of the Minneapolis-based Carlson Companies, Inc., has its roots in the oldest travel agency in the United States. Before it was acquired by Carlson Companies in 1979, it was known as Ask Mr. Foster Travel, a travel business founded in 1888 by Ward G. Foster in St. Augustine, Florida.

Wagonlit Travel, a unit of the Paris-based Accor Group, began taking care of clients' travel arrangements in 1872. Its founder, Belgian innovator Georges Nagelmackers, went on to establish one of Europe's most famous rail lines, the Orient Express.

While the two agencies have joined forces in the travel business, they continue to operate as core units of Carlson Companies and the Accor Group. For that reason, Carlson Wagonlit maintains two headquarters, one in Minneapolis and one in Paris.

Despite its already huge size, the travel agency is still far from reaching its full growth potential, according to Carlson Wagonlit officials. Currently, it is actively looking to acquire or affiliate with existing travel agencies in the Asia-Pacific region, South America, and Australia.

Incidentally, the best time to make a conference call between Chicago, London, and Moscow might be 8 a.m. Chicago time — which is 2 p.m. in London and 5 p.m. in Moscow. At those hours, all three colleagues would likely be in their offices. Arriving at the solution was easy, thanks to an infographic created by Carlson Wagonlit Travel that helps its clients navigate through the maze of 24 different time zones around the world.

TOP PHOTO: ELEANOR JACOBSON, A MINNEAPOLIS CARLSON WAGONLIT TRAVEL AGENT, IS IMMERSED IN 4,100 GLOBE BALLS, ONE FOR EACH OF THE COMPANY'S 4,100 LOCATIONS AROUND THE WORLD. BOTTOM PHOTO: SHOWN IS A CARLSON WAGONLIT OFFICE IN PARIS.

Sheraton Gateway Suites
Chicago O'Hare Airport

Elegant amenities, refined hospitality

Sheraton Gateway Suites — conveniently located just five minutes from Chicago O'Hare International Airport — stands proud and tall like the beaming father of a newborn baby.

Indeed, this 11-story suburban-Rosemont hotel, known as Embassy Suites O'Hare before the Boston-based ITT Sheraton acquired it in February 1994, has the look and feel of a newborn.

Thanks to a $4.9 million head-to-toe renovation by Sheraton, this structure has been transformed into one of the finest and most modern hotel properties in the Chicago area.

As a result of the remodeling, each of the Sheraton Gateway's 300 spacious guest suites has new carpeting, new wallpaper, new furniture, and upgraded bathrooms. Even the artwork hanging on the walls in the

rooms and along the open corridors surrounding the hotel's atrium is new.

The public areas of the hotel have been redone as well. On the ground floor, in the center of the lobby's atrium is the Luna Grille, a wonderful new restaurant, and an adjoining piano lounge with the relaxing ambience of an outdoor cafe.

For those in search of a little more excitement, 72 West Lounge, located just off the lobby, is just the place. This lively bistro features light snacks as well as a variety of beers, wines, and Chicago-style cocktails.

Other Sheraton Gateway amenities include an indoor pool, a whirlpool, a sauna, and a workout area. And for real physical-fitness buffs, hotel guests enjoy privileges at the Willow Creek Fitness Club, located right next door.

Many Sheraton Gateway guests are businesspeople with very active schedules, and the hotel offers virtually everything to accommodate their needs. Each floor of the hotel con-

tains a boardroom complete with audio and visual equipment. In addition, a ground-floor business center offers fax, computer, and transcription services.

Location, as they say, is everything, and the Sheraton Gateway is only minutes away from the Rosemont Convention Center, the new Rosemont Theatre, and the Horizon stadium, which hosts concerts, college basketball games, ice hockey, and professional indoor soccer matches. Downtown Chicago and the whole metropolitan area are within easy reach via nearby expressways and tollways.

Put it all together, and it's easy to understand why Sheraton Gateway Suites was recently awarded the prestigious Four Diamond hotel property rating. This hotel is one of the top Chicago-area destinations for discriminating travelers.

Indeed, what better place to land, whether the purpose of one's visit to Chicago is business or pleasure.

ABOVE: THE SHERATON GATEWAY SUITES' GRAND BALLROOM, WHICH CAN ACCOMMODATE AS MANY AS 500 PEOPLE, BRINGS ELEGANCE AND STYLE TO EVERY OCCASION. LEFT: THE ATRIUM'S ALFRESCO-STYLE DINING AND PIANO LOUNGE AREA OFFERS AN INVITING SETTING FOR GUESTS TO ENJOY SPECIALLY PREPARED ENTREES FROM THE LUNA GRILLE.

Corporate Sponsors

....

The following companies and organizations have made a valuable commitment to the quality of this publication. Cherbo Publishing Group and Chicago O'Hare International Airport gratefully acknowledge their participation in *Chicago O'Hare International Airport: World's Busiest, World's Best.*

**Airport Owners
Representatives, 123**
Chicago O'Hare International Airport
AMF O'Hare, P.O. Box 66790
Chicago, IL 60666
Phone: (773) 894-3751
Fax: (773) 686-1721

Allstate Insurance Company, 126
2775 Sanders Road, Suite F-3
Northbrook, IL 60062
Phone: (847) 402-8941
Fax: (847) 326-7515

American Airlines, 90
Chicago O'Hare International Airport
P.O. Box 66065
Chicago, IL 60666
Phone: (800) 433-7300
http://www.americanair.com

Ameritech Corp., 108
30 South Wacker Drive, Suite 3400
Chicago, IL 60606
Phone: (800) 257-0902
Fax: (312) 207-1601
http://www.ameritech.com

Aon Risk Services, 128
123 North Wacker Drive
Chicago, IL 60606
Phone: (312) 701-4000
Fax: (312) 701-4143 or (312) 701-4144
E-mail: web_master@aon.com
http://www.aon.com

Best Western Midway Hotel, 132
1600 East Oakton Street
Elk Grove Village, IL 60007
Phone: (847) 981-0010
Fax: (847) 364-7365

British Airways, 100
75-20 Astoria Boulevard
Jackson Heights, NY 11370
Phone: (718) 397-4000
Reservations: (800) 528-1234
Fax: (718) 397-4290
http://www.british-airways.com

Carlson Wagonlit Travel, 134
P.O. Box 59159
Minneapolis, MN 55459
Phone: (612) 449-2488
Fax: (612) 449-1288
http://www.travel.carlson.com
(leisure travel)
http://www.carlsonwagonlit.com
(business travel)

Chicago Aviation Partners, 105
Chicago O'Hare International Airport
International Terminal
AMF O'Hare, P.O. Box 66182
Chicago, IL 60666-0182
Phone: (312) 894-9595
Fax: (312) 894-9599

China Eastern Airlines, 98
551 North Michigan Avenue, Suite 200
Chicago, IL 60611
Phone: (312) 329-0100
Fax: (312) 329-0080

HNTB Corporation, 122
111 North Canal Street, Suite 880
Chicago, IL 60606-7252
Phone: (312) 930-9119
Fax: (312) 930-9063
E-mail: gstyler@hntb.com
http://www.hntb.com

Hopkins & Sutter, 130
Three First National Plaza, Suite 4300
Chicago, IL 60602
Phone: (312) 558-6600
Fax: (312) 558-6538
http://www.hopsut.com

Hudson General LLC, 94
10600 West Higgins Road, Suite 610
Rosemont, IL 60018
Phone: (847) 298-6140
Fax: (847) 298-6769

K-Five Construction Corp., 120
13769 Main Street
Lemont, IL 60439
Phone: (630) 257-5600
Fax: (630) 257-6788

Korean Air, 96
230 North Michigan Avenue, Suite 400
Chicago, IL 60601
Phone: (312) 558-9300
Fax: (312) 558-5006

Landrum & Brown, 112
1021 West Adams Street
Chicago, IL 60607
Phone: (312) 421-0500
Fax: (312) 421-6171
http://www.landrum-brown.com

LOT Polish Airlines, 99
333 North Michigan Avenue, Suite 921
Chicago, IL 60601
Phone: Reservations: (312) 236-3388
            Administration: (312) 236-5501
Fax: (312) 236-5025
E-mail: webmaster@Lot.com
http://www.lot.com

Ogilvy Adams & Rinehart, 129
900 North Michigan Avenue,
Suite 2750
Chicago, IL 60611
Phone: (312) 988-3801
Fax: (312) 988-2683
E-mail: Marilou_von_Ferstel1%OAR@
            notes.worldcom.com
http://www.@notes.worldcom.com

O'Hare Hilton Hotel, 104
Chicago O'Hare International Airport
P.O. Box 66414
Chicago, IL 60666
Phone: (773) 686-8000
Fax: (773) 601-2339
http://www.hilton.com

Ricondo & Associates, Inc., 116
20 North Clark Street, Suite 1250
Chicago, IL 60602-4111
Phone: (312) 606-0611
Fax: (312) 606-0706

**Rust Environment &
Infrastructure Inc., 124**
111 North Canal Street, Suite 305
Chicago, IL 60606
Phone: (312) 902-7100
Fax: (312) 902-7099

Bibliography

Chapter One

Chicago American, March 1963.

Chicago Association of Commerce. "Chicago Facts," 1927.

Chicago Sun Times. "Bessie Coleman" story, 19 March 1995.

Chicago Tribune. May 1919; May 1926; November 1931; July 1943; August 1945; September 1949; March 1963.

Clayton, John. *Illinois Fact Book and Historical Almanac, 1673–1968.* Carbondale, Ill.: Southern Illinois University Press, 1970.

Department of Aviation, City of Chicago. Archival materials.

Heise, Kenan. *Is There Only One Chicago?* N.p.: Westover Publishing, 1973.

Journals of the Proceedings of the City Council of the City of Chicago. Chicago, Ill.: 1926, 1945, 1946, 1949, 1950, 1990.

Roseberry, C. R. *The Challenging Skies.* N.p.: Doubleday & Company, 1966.

WMAQ-TV (NBC), "Bessie Coleman" biography. 6 March 1990, video-cassette.

Wray, James R. "Atlas of Chicago Municipal Airport." Dissertation, Department of Geography, University of Chicago, 1948.

Chapter Two

Bergreen, Laurence. *Capone: The Man and the Era.* N.p.: Simon & Schuster, 1994.

Bransfield, Lt. Comdr. Chuck (U.S. Navy). Interview by the author, November 1996.

Burke, Edward. Speech before the Glenview Chamber of Commerce, March 1995; interview by the author, May 1995.

Chicago Daily News, 1939–1961.

Chicago Herald American, 1965.

Chicago Sun Times, 1948–1960.

Chicago Tribune, 1948–1960.

Department of Aviation, City of Chicago. Archival materials.

Doherty, Richard P. *Origin & Development of Chicago — O'Hare International Airport.* Ann Arbor, Mich.: University Microfilms, 1971.

Hoellen, John. Interview by the author, August 1995.

Journals of the Proceedings of the City Council of the City of Chicago. Chicago, Ill.: 1945, 1946, 1949, 1950, 1990.

Kokendorfer, A.A. Interview, 1962.

Schoenberg, Robert J. *Mr. Capone: The Real and Complete Story of Al Capone.* N.p.: William Morrow & Co., 1992.

Schultz, Harold. Interview by the author, August 1995.

Chapter Three

Brodherson, David. "All Airplanes Lead to Chicago." In *Chicago Architecture and Design, 1923–1993,* edited by John Zukowsky. N.p.: Prestel, The Art Institute of Chicago, 1993.

Chicago Daily News, 13 June 1966.

Chicago Sun Times, 11 January 1962.

Chicago Tribune, 1 January 1962.

Clayton, John. *Illinois Fact Book and Historical Almanac, 1673–1968.* Carbondale, Ill.: Southern Illinois University Press, 1970.

Darrow, Donna. Interview by the author, October 1995.

Department of Aviation, City of Chicago. Archival documents.

Journals of the Proceedings of the City Council of the City of Chicago. Chicago, Ill.: n.d.

Mannix, Ed. Interview by the author, September 1995.

Martelle, Ed. Interview by the author, November 1995.

O'Connor, Len. Comments to the author, May 1966.

Population and Statistics. Government documents, Evanston, Ill: Northwestern University, 1950.

U.S. Bureau of the Census. *Population and Statistics.* Prepared by the Geography Division in cooperation with the Housing Division, Bureau of the Census, Washington, D.C., 1990.

Chapter Four

American Institute of Architects, Chicago. Archival materials.

The Art Institute of Chicago, Public Relations Department. Archival materials.

Brodherson, David. "All Airplanes Lead to Chicago." In *Chicago Architecture and Design, 1923–1993,* edited by John Zukowsky. N.p.: Prestel, The Art Institute of Chicago, 1993.

Chicago Association of Commerce. Brochure, 1945.

Chicago Convention and Tourism Bureau. Tourism materials and press kit, 1996.

Chicago District Golfer Magazine, January/February 1996.

Chicago Symphony Orchestra, Communications Department. Promotional materials.

Chicago Tribune, 1990–1996.

Department of Aviation, City of Chicago. "Chicago Airport System Annual Reports." Chicago, Ill.: 1992–1993, 1993–1994.

Department of Aviation, City of Chicago. "Chicago O'Hare International Airport, Terminal 5." Chicago, Ill.: n.d.

Fagan, Mary Francis. Interview by the author, December 1995; American Airlines archival materials.

Hansen, Barbara. United Airlines archival materials.

Kelly, Mayor Edward J. Letter, 1945; City of Chicago archival files.

McCormick Place/Navy Pier, Public Affairs. Promotional materials, 1996.

Population and Statistics. Government documents, Evanston, Ill: Northwestern University, 1950.

Rosemont Convention Center. Promotional materials. Rosemont, Ill.: 1996.

WMAQ-TV (NBC), "International Terminal" report. May 1993, videocassette.

Chapter Five

Chicago Sun Times, 1 March 1996.

Chicago Tribune, "Chicago's Top 100," May 1995; 1995–1996.

Daniels, Lee. Illinois House of Representatives archival materials.

Department of Aviation, City of Chicago. Records.

Murphy, Barrett. Interview with the author, October 1995. Interview in *The New York Times,* 3 February 1996.

Population and Statistics. Government documents, Evanston, Ill: Northwestern University, 1950.

Sandburg, Carl. "Chicago." In *Contemporary Trends, American Literature Since 1900,* edited by John H. Nelson and Oscar Cargill. New York: The MacMillan Co., 1947.

U.S. Bureau of the Census. *Population and Statistics.* Prepared by the Geography Division in cooperation with the Housing Division, Bureau of the Census, Washington, D.C., 1990.

Wall Street Journal, n.d.

PHOTO BY PETER J. SCHULZ, CITY OF CHICAGO, DEPT. OF AVIATION

Index

Index continued